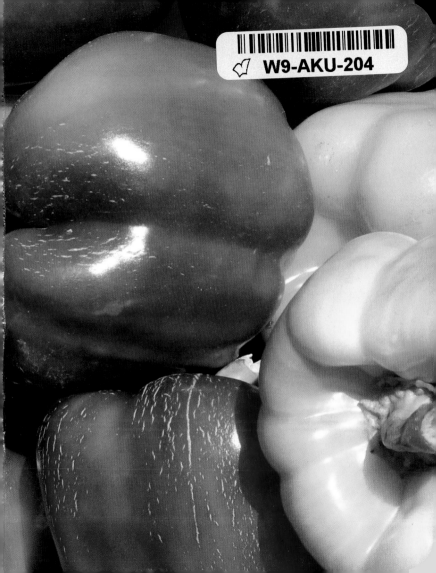

Markets of New York City
A Guide to the Best Artisan,
Farmer, Food and Flea Markets

Markets of New York City

A Guide to the Best Artisan, Farmer, Food and Flea Markets

Karen E. Seiger

The Little Bookroom
New York

Book design: Lauren Ruggeri

Library of Congress Cataloging-in-Publication Data

Seiger, Karen E.
Markets of New York City : a guide to the best artisan, farmer, food, and flea
markets / by Karen E. Seiger ; photographs by Karen E. Seiger.
p. cm.
ISBN 978-1-892145-85-7 (alk. paper)
1. Markets--New York (State)--New York--Guidebooks. 2. Artisans--New York
(State)--New York--Guidebooks. 3. Farmers' markets--New York (State)--New
York--Guidebooks. 4. Flea markets--New York (State)--New York--Guidebooks.
5. New York (N.Y.)--Guidebooks. I. Title.
HF5472.U7N64 2010
381'.1097471--dc22

Additional photo credits: pages 71-73 (Digby & Iona, Clo Studio, Charm NYC,
Arza, full page) James Wesolowski, Page 71 (Nature vs. Future) Simon Gerzina,
Page 81 (Jennifer Stewart) James Wesolowski, Page 87 (She Hit Pause Studios)
Matt Schwartz, Page 122 Ken Blauvelt, Page 128 (Ian Lander) Casey Leigh
Goldsmith, Page 133 (Linda B. Cromer) Linda B. Cromer, Pages 134, 136 and 146
James Wesolowski, Page 138 Miguel Ullivarri, Page 144 Upsilon Ventures

Published by The Little Bookroom
435 Hudson Street, Suite 300
New York NY 10014
editorial@littlebookroom.com
www.littlebookroom.com

10 9 8 7 6 5 4 3 2 1

To my darling husband James
and to my mother Haydee, who first
took me to the markets of the world.

Contents

Introduction

Wherever I travel, the first places I seek out are the local markets. To me, markets are the most fascinating and accessible places to learn about a culture and connect with its people. My family spent many holiday seasons in Mexico City, and I have vivid childhood memories of the sights and smells of the sprawling La Merced market. While working in Lima, Peru, I had a rare day all to myself, and $20 in my pocket. I came home from an artists market in a park with a sunburn and twenty beautiful watercolor paintings, now hanging in my hallway. My mother has a masterfully hand-crocheted, queen-size comforter on her bed that I found at a crafts market in Swaziland. Whenever my husband and I are in Paris, we buy fresh fruit and vegetables at the local farmers markets, as well as delicious cheeses, pastries, flowers, and sometimes a perfectly roasted chicken. I could go on and on, but the point is that markets are places to shop, eat, meet people, and maybe find a treasure to last you a lifetime— or at least through lunchtime.

The artisan, farmer, food, and flea markets of New York are no exception. They have always been an important part of life here, and they remain so today. There are more than fifty farmers markets each week in the five boroughs, all loaded with fresh locally grown produce, as well as breads, honey, wine, and many other wonderful treats. Upcoming trends in design, fashion, and art can all be found at the artisan and designer markets. The quality and creativity of the merchandise is unparalleled. The city's flea markets continue to offer unusual items and plenty of fantastic bargains.

I admire people who make their living following their creative passions, be they artists, farmers, or collectors. There is something very special about buying an object directly from the person who made it or cultivated it. I also love the idea that most of these markets are built from the ground up in the wee hours of the morning and then disappear at the end of the day. Spend the day strolling through the markets, exploring New York's neighborhoods, and eating delicious food, and you have yourself a perfect adventure in the city.

About This Guide

This book is a guide to the traditional, charming, and edgy markets in New York City. For centuries, people have been meeting at markets to buy and sell their goods. New York's markets maintain that tradition. The people, products, and places described in this guidebook reflect the fact that New Yorkers still value the traditional kinds of markets where you can find a bargain or a treasure, and connect with people, which is not always easy to do in a fast-paced city like this one.

I have tried to provide the most comprehensive information possible about the best markets in town. The majority of the markets mentioned are long established, although there are some exciting new ones as well. I have highlighted some of my favorite artists and vendors to give you a flavor of what you may find at each market. Many of the markets have food vendors that sell a variety of delicious savory and sweet treats, and I have included information about them also. For markets that do not have food vendors, I recommend that you ask for suggestions from the vendors themselves and your fellow shoppers. I guarantee that you are never too far from the perfect slice of pizza or, these days, a delectable frosted cupcake.

Based on my knowledge and sources, the most successful and

dynamic markets of all kinds are to be found in Manhattan and Brooklyn. There are several farmers markets in Queens and the Bronx. However, most of these markets are quite small. There is only one farmers market each week on Staten Island, although there are plans to launch a second one. These smaller markets provide great value and service to the surrounding communities, but they are not yet large enough to be recommended as destinations. That said, I have highlighted two quite special farmers markets in these boroughs to give you an idea of how important they can be to the neighborhoods they serve, Poe Park in the Bronx (page 243) and Jackson Heights in Queens (page 249).

By their very nature, markets are always changing, whether the vendors, the location, or the operating hours. In the artisan and flea markets, the vendors change from week to week, which is part of their charm and a good reason to keep going back. New markets are launched every year. I aim to try and keep up with these changes on my blog, so please check there for updates (www.marketsofnewyork.com).

The Markets

This guide is not a comprehensive listing of all the markets in New York City. It is my attempt to identify the best ones. New markets pop up every month; some will survive, and some will not. I have included markets that are likely to be around for years to come. Many have an extraordinarily wide range of items for sale, and others are quite focused on a particular type of item, such as fashion or food. The descriptions and photos of each market will give you a good idea of what you will find behind the doors, fences, or tent flaps at each one.

The guide covers several types of markets:

Artisan Markets

There are many exciting markets featuring some of the city's most talented and cutting-edge designers and craftspeople. Many fine artists, including painters, sculptors, and photographers take part in these markets as well, selling their work directly to the public, rather than through an agent or gallery. I have also included several seasonal artisan markets, as well as the major holiday markets, some of which have participants from across the country.

Farmers Markets

Whether you live in New York or you are a visitor, you can take advantage of the colorful farmers markets all over town. In addition to the freshest seasonal produce, the markets offer many other products. You can find bread and artisanal cheeses at most of the green markets, which make for a perfect picnic in a park. The larger farmers markets, such as the one at Union Square, have a wider variety of items, including wine, flowers, canned goods, honeys, and more. If you go early enough, you may just bump into your favorite celebrity chef, many of whom shop for their daily menu items at the green markets.

Food Purveyor Markets

In the 1940s, Mayor Fiorello La Guardia moved all the pushcart vendors off the streets and into several indoor markets to make room for the increasing number of cars in the city. Several of these markets, including the Essex Street, Moore Street, and Arthur Avenue markets, are included in the guide. Two modern versions of indoor food markets, Chelsea and Grand Central markets, are included as well. The New

Amsterdam Market for local food purveyors has been held for several years at the former site of the historic Fulton Fish Market, and the hope is that it finds a permanent home there.

Flea Markets

People may say that the East Coast is "shopped out" for antiques and fleas, but I have found it to be quite the opposite. You can still find wonderful items for sale at places like the Hell's Kitchen Flea Market, the GreenFlea, or the Antiques Garage. Whether you are looking for watches, furniture, decorative items, vintage clothing, or any other kind of artifact, you can still find wonderful treasures at these markets. Dealers and collectors get there very early for the best selection, and bargain hunters fare best at the end of the day.

Most of the markets in this guide are not strictly one type of market. Often artisan markets combine with flea markets. You will also find farmers markets right near artisan and flea markets, such as McCarren Park in Brooklyn and Columbus Avenue in Manhattan. The East 67th Street Flea Market has several farm stands incorporated into the market itself. Additionally, although the farmers markets do sell local fruits and vegetables, you will also find many other food products, including canned goods, jams, baked goods, honey, beef jerky, cheeses, and much more. So, although this book covers four distinct market types—artisan, farmer, food, and flea—you will often find some combination of all four in one venue.

Food at the Markets

The vast majority of the markets listed in this guide have food that you can eat on the spot. The Brooklyn Flea markets boast some of the most innovative and delicious food in the city. You can have a healthy lunch at all of the farmers markets, buying a loaf of bread, some zingy artisanal cheese, and perfect peaches for dessert. You can even get a bottle of wine or hard cider at the larger markets.

For the few markets that don't have food available inside, well, you are in New York City, which means you are never far from a deli, a hot dog vendor, or some of the finest restaurants in the world. Ask the vendors where they eat, and trust their judgment.

A Word About Bargains and Bargaining

The word "bargain" means different things to different people. A bargain for one person may be a pair of "previously loved" Prada sandals in great condition for $20, or an $18 hand-crocheted red beret. For someone else, it might be a $600 antique Edison phonograph in working condition at the Hell's Kitchen Flea Market or $50 for a lace lingerie set at the Young Designers Market that retails in the best boutiques for $300. For me, three mini-cupcakes for $2 make my day.

I have mixed feelings about bargaining, although it is practiced world-wide. Artisans, bakers, and dealers work painstakingly to bring their wonderful and unique products to us in the markets. In general, their pricing is far below what you would pay in a shop. The flea market vendors are more used to bargaining than artists or farmers are, but bear in mind that they have to buy their merchandise and work outdoors in all kinds of weather to make a living.

The general rule is to be reasonable and respectful with your offer. If a vendor is asking $50 for an item, don't offer $5. Many vendors have told me that the best way to come to mutually agreeable terms is to ask the vendor for the best price they can give you. You usually have more leverage if you buy multiple items from the same vendor. If you like the price, then pull out your wallet. If you don't, walk away. No harm, no foul.

The bottom line is that you should be prepared for anything at these markets. Because there is such a wide variety of items, prices vary accordingly. In the very likely event that you find something you can't leave behind, the vendors will be able to point you towards the nearest ATM and hold the item until you return. It's not a bad idea to bring a credit card—most vendors are cash-only, but some do accept plastic.

Two Important Lessons

There are two important lessons that I have learned the hard way and that I must share with you:

Lesson #1: If you like it, buy it. Now. In New York, there's not much time for consideration because the next person will step in and buy your item while you are still thinking about it. Many, if not most, of the items in these markets are one-of-a-kind, so if you really want something, buy it with no regrets.

Lesson #2: Set a budget for the day and stick to it. I have seen items in the markets ranging from fifty cents for an old scarf to $17,000 for a vintage diamond and emerald ring. If you set a budget for yourself, you do not have to decide if you can afford an item; it is either within your budget or it is not.

Do's and Don'ts When Exploring New York City

New York is a "grand experiment" where 8.2 million people live together in the most densely populated city in the U.S. This city has been around— and growing—since 1625, so we must be doing something right. Despite New York's "anything goes" appeal, there are in fact some rules and behaviors that keep the place running. You can slip right into the flow by adhering to a few basic rules.

Be courteous. Always hold doors and offer your seat on the bus or subway for people who are elderly, handicapped, pregnant, or carrying children (men and women).

Know before you go. Spending a day wandering and getting lost in the city is a perfectly wonderful thing to do, but if you have a specific destination in mind, look at a map to figure out how to get there before you step out the door. Subway maps are free at any station with an attended kiosk.

Figure out the compass points. You definitely need to know which way is north, south, east, or west in order to get anywhere in New York. New Yorkers use landmarks, usually big buildings, to find their way. We used to use the 110-story towers of the World Trade Center as a compass to locate south. Now we have to rely on the position of the sun. No kidding. If you can't actually see the sun (buildings, cloudy weather), ask for directions. It's okay. Most people will be glad to help.

Don't cause a pile-up. Start by thinking of New York City sidewalks as high-speed superhighways. We walk everywhere, and we move fast. Like cars, pedestrians have their lanes on the sidewalks. If you get out of your lane, or stop dead in your tracks to check your phone messages or look at a map, you will get a few choice words spat at you at best or cause a pile-up at worst. A group of people, or even just two, can block an entire city sidewalk. If you need to stop for any reason, move over to the edge of the sidewalk to let people pass.

Follow cab-hailing etiquette. If someone is on the corner where you need a cab, never walk half a block in front of him or her to catch the next cab before they do. If you wait your turn, your cab will come. I realize that this rule is hard to enforce in Midtown, where someone is always a half block ahead of you, but there are enough cabs for everyone. Alternatively, you can always take the subway, which is usually the faster option anyway.

Icon Guide

artisan   flea   food   farmer

Artisan and Flea Markets

Permanent and Semi-Permanent Markets
Manhattan

Antiques Garage

112 West 25th Street (Sixth Ave. / Seventh Ave.)
Saturday & Sunday, 9 am to 5 pm
1, C, E, F, V to 23rd Street
www.hellskitchenfleamarket.com
(Note: The Antiques Garage and the Hell's Kitchen
Flea Market are under the same management.)

During the week, New Yorkers walk right past this dingy parking garage without giving it a second glance. But on Saturday and Sunday, they can't ignore the steamer trunks, rocking chairs, and maybe even a zebra pelt or two that spill onto the sidewalk out front. These unexpected items mark the entrance to the Antiques Garage, a market that has been held for several years in this functioning garage that clears out the cars each weekend to make way for the dealers.

Once your eyes adjust to being inside, the Garage springs to life with millions of items displayed on two entire floors. It is a wonderful place to spend an afternoon browsing through the numerous and diverse booths, escaping from the weather, be it hot, cold, or rainy. The vendors are knowledgeable and willing to chat with you about their wares, the history of the market, and pretty much any other subject. Some of the dealers come and go, but many of them are here every weekend, and have been for years.

Much of the merchandise comes from the estates of the wonderfully interesting and eclectic denizens of New York City. Dealers have told me about Albert Einstein autographs, Audubon prints, as well as Diane

Arbus and Annie Leibovitz photographs that have come through the market recently and sold for a relative pittance. Feel free to talk with other shoppers about their best finds. If you are looking for something specific, ask around. People will point you in the right direction if they can.

Like the other markets in New York, you may bump into a fashion model buying 1960s go-go boots, a designer looking at vintage styles for inspiration, a decorator carting off a crystal chandelier, and maybe even a celebrity or two. Catherine Deneuve and Diane Keaton have been known to stop by the Garage on occasion.

There are no food vendors in the Garage but there are several delis and coffee shops right around the corner on Sixth Avenue. For a more substantial meal, walk over to Eighth Avenue, where there are lovely small restaurants.

Lulu's Vintage Lovelies Lulu's selection focuses mainly on the sixties, seventies, and eighties, but she also has designs from as far back as the 1890s. You may find a sixties orange mini-dress with a huge round belt buckle, a vivid Pucci lingerie set, or a vintage Gucci bag in perfect condition. Contestants from Project Runway stop by for inspiration, as do many famous designers, including Betsey Johnson. The labels you may come across at Lulu's include Christian Dior, Valentino, Bergdorf Goodman, and more.

Deborah Leonard Collection Ms. Leonard is a vintage vendor of high-quality estate jewelry and clothing. She sells finely detailed pairs of lamp and other pieces for your living room décor. Leonard is also the vendor liaison for the market, and knows all about it, so feel free to ask her where to look for specific items.

Bengay Diop African Art Bengay Diop has a remarkable collection of African art and artifacts in a far corner of the Garage, including masks, statuettes, and large hand-carved wooden bowl sets that interior decorators are drawn to. Diop has Bakota pieces from Gabon, Dogon objects from Mali, bronzes from Nigeria, and more; if you are looking for something specific, Diop can arrange to show you pieces from his nearby storage space. Prices range from $50 to $20,000.

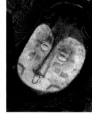

Hobbit Rare Books & Prints On the second floor you'll find several long tables covered with antiquarian books, prints, and original works of art. Dealer Arby Rolband has thousands of architectural, geographic, and natural history prints, and only a fraction of them are out on the tables. His collections are a favorite among art dealers and collectors; he also sells to decorators and designers from around the world. If you need an historic map of South America or an old botanical print, come and see Arby.

Oddball Americana A favorite of New York's prop scouts, set designers, and decorators, Janet West finds and sells eccentric items from all periods of U.S. history, including toys, board and card games, furniture, and decorative items. You might find a collection of wedding cake toppers from the early twentieth century, a tin tub full of colorful rubber duckies from the twenties, or a box of Mickey Mouse ornaments from the thirties; have fun rummaging through paper dolls, dominos, jacks, and more.

Gary Lickver Pottery & Carnival Glass Gary Lickver travels from San Diego to the Antiques Garage several times a year. If you are lucky enough to find him, spend time examining his collections of Carnival, Northwood, and Fenton glass, as well as the many pieces of Meissen pottery. Roseville pottery, with its rich colors and beautiful patterns, is one of Mr. Lickver's strong suits. His cases of silver and enameled souvenir spoons are as fascinating as they are beautiful.

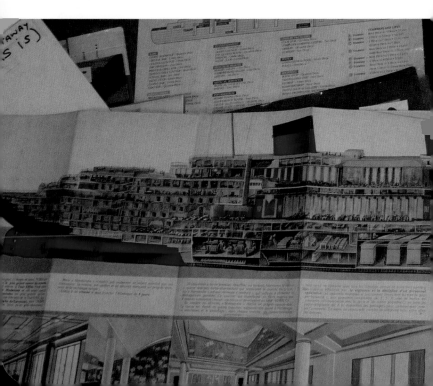

Bakelite and Ocean Liner Memorabilia This dealer is an excellent source for Bakelite, the highly collectible vintage plastic, as well as beautiful contemporary French jewelry made from modern celluloid. At the booth you'll also find some remarkable examples of ship memorabilia, including menus, lapel pins, brochures, posters, and postcards from historic ocean liners such as the *Normandie*, whose artifacts are among the most collectible.

Artists at Union Square

Union Square (East 14th St. to E. 17th St. where Broadway,
Park Ave. South, Fourth Ave. and University Pl. converge)
Daily 10 am to 8 pm, depending on the weather
4, 5, 6, L, N, Q, R, W to 14th Street-Union Square

Union Square always seems to have something interesting going on, be it a concert, a snowboarding exhibition, the greenmarket, or a Free Tibet protest. It is also the year-round home for New York artists who sell their handicrafts at the south and west sides of the square.

This particular artist market is unusual because the artisans can simply show up and set up their tables—they only need a Tax ID number. Unlike most of the other markets in the city, there is no management organization. As a result, you'll find a vast variety of artists and merchandise.

Union Square has a long history as a gathering place for political activists, and today you'll find plenty of political T-shirts in support of the environment, Native American rights, and other causes alongside jewelers, photographers, sculptors, hat makers, and even personal advisors and tarot card readers.

Weekends are the busiest, especially on Saturdays with the Union Square Greenmarket on the west and north sides of the Square, but you'll find interesting artisans on weekdays as well.

 **Severyn Hand Printed/Hand Dyed Shirts** (www. severyn.com) Artist Severyn's colorful and eye-catching shirts feature extremely detailed silk-screened designs inspired by nature. Some are tie-dyed, others are simple colored tees.

 **Little Dipper Castings** (www.littledipperscastings.com) A relative newcomer to Union Square, Little Dipper Castings sells jewelry made from pewter casts of unusual items. The Specimens Collection includes pewter necklaces and earrings based on a rat snake vertebra, a prehistoric shark tooth, or a monkey finger bone, to mention just a few inspirations. Little Dipper also makes jewelry based on more traditional motifs, such as a sand dollar, a starfish, and rope knots.

 1178 Designs (www.1178designs.com) The two French designers associated with 1178 create beautiful, colorful glass art, including jewelry, bowls, lamps, and more, in a variety of styles. Silk-screened mosaic glass bowls with images of "famous people" and quotations are two of their signature items.

Pangaea Paper You may have seen Pangaea Paper's beautiful journals, albums, frames, and other gifts in stores such as World Market. The products are handmade in Bali using organic materials such as leaves, seeds, and wood.

Soigné T-Shirts Maybe it was the bright green snake around the neck of Soigné's scarlet T-shirt that first caught my eye. The artist's bug-eyed monsters, animals, and insects are funny and colorful. Each one is hand-painted, some on tie-dyed T-shirts.

Cartoonist El Naide Also known as Jairo Barragán, El Naide's cartoons are clever, funny, and sometimes political. One drawing, "The City that Never Sleeps," depicts New York's skyscrapers with eyes instead of windows. Naide's cartoons have been published in *The New York Times* and other publications.

Jongo Jananda This painter lives on an island in Micronesia but spends time in New York. His paintings feature humorous characters demonstrating yoga poses; aluminum foil incorporated into the borders provides a metallic contrast to the colorful images.

Billy's Antiques and Props

76 East Houston Street (Elizabeth St. / Bowery)
Tuesday to Sunday, 1 pm to 8 pm, weather permitting;
Mondays by appointment
B, D, F, V to Broadway-Lafayette Street; 6 to Bleecker Street
www.billysantiques.com

You can't miss Billy's Antiques and Props' big green tent. Billy started selling antiques and unusual items in 1986 when the Bowery was far from the chi-chi nightspot it recently has become. He also provides props for movies, plays, and events.

The large tent is not weatherized—it's very hot in the summer and freezing in the winter—but the merchandise is eclectic and fascinating. You might find an antique gypsy fortune teller carnival booth or a cigar store wooden Indian. Deer heads are mounted on the fence above used bikes, armchairs, and steamer trunks. Billy's once had a set of plastic arms and hands with serious wounds; they were used for teaching traumatic wound treatment, but I thought they would have been perfect for my next Halloween party.

Billy is the only dealer authorized to sell authentic New York City subway signs that become obsolete when a line is changed or eliminated. You can pick up an authentic World Trade Center sign for $250.

In good weather, chances are you'll find Billy sitting on an armchair on the sidewalk with his dog Kill Joy, in the shade of his famous nine-foot-tall Santa Claus.

East 67th Street Market

Public School 183
Robert Louis Stevenson Elementary School
East 66th & 67th Street (First Ave. / York Ave.)
Saturday 6 am to 5 pm
6 to 68th Street-Hunter College
www.east67thstreetmarket.org

Nicely housed in Public School 183, the East 67th Street Market has vendors both indoors and out. The outdoor vendors set up their tents and tables on the school's playground and small running track, while the indoor vendors arrange their wares on cafeteria tables. There are vendors on the East 67th Street sidewalk outside the schoolyard fence who are also officially part of the flea market.

Fees paid by the vendors to participate in the market every Saturday go to support the educational activities of the school. This market has been ongoing since 1979.

This market is smaller than the Hell's Kitchen and the GreenFlea markets, but do not let that dissuade you from spending your time browsing the tables here. Dealers sell antique furniture, decorative pieces, jewelry, and more, and several farmers sell fruit, vegetables, and flowers. All kinds of food are readily available to snack on from market vendors, who all must be certified by the City of New York to sell edible items.

Rosalind's As You Liked It Rosalind Harris, who you may have seen as Tzeitel in the movie "Fiddler on the Roof," says, "I have something for everyone!" She sells high-quality vintage jewelry, from beautiful sterling silver baubles to magnificent, gem-encrusted statement pieces. Whether you spend $50 or $17,000, her prices are well below retail. Some of her most colorful jewels are from the 1960s; she also has a wonderful collection of 1940s Hollywood glamour jewelry. She counts Catherine Zeta-Jones and Bernadette Peters among her long-time clients. You also can find her at the GreenFlea market on Sundays.

Eyeware by Sarita Sarita is a professional optician. She sells only "dead stock" frames—vintage pieces that have never been sold. Her collection ranges from 1880s wire readers to stunning Jackie O styles. Funky 1980s frames sit alongside 1950s cat-eyes. She supplies sunglasses to many Broadway costume designers. Customers over the years have included Donald Trump, Walter Cronkite, Paul Simon, and Hilary Swank. She also makes jewelry from vintage stones—pick up some peepers and add a chunky necklace to complete your look.

Indian Décor Nirmal Singh's sumptuous silk duvet covers, pillow shams, coverlets, and throw pillows come in rich oranges, pinks, blues, and greens with golden silk embroidery. He also sells colorful door hangings, which are said to bring good luck to each room in your house. If you need even more good luck, Singh also offers various sizes of wall hangings with intricately adorned elephants and the elephant god Ganesh, both said to bring good fortune, wisdom, and removal of obstacles.

Interesting Old Things Interesting Old Things has a delightful collection of antique bits and baubles. You can find many one-of-a-kind pieces in the cases: tiny bears and small porcelain dolls, a miniature sewing kit and thimble housed in a brass walnut with a little hinge and clasp, intricately decorated sterling silver sewing scissors, and antique pocket compasses.

Paul Craffey (www.paulcraffey.com) Paul Craffey has a beautiful set-up in the corner of the cafeteria where you can gaze at—and try on—his remarkable estate jewelry. He may have a gigantic amethyst ring or a deep blue lapis lazuli pinkie ring; one Saturday I saw a vintage Cartier watch from the estate of Edith Beale of "Grey Gardens" fame. Craffey also has a first-class collection of silver and turquoise Native American jewelry, and, on the walls behind his cases, vintage magazines and photographs of celebrities such as Marilyn Monroe.

Nina Grand World Piece Clothing designer Nina Grand makes her brightly hued women's clothing from Indian silk and cotton. One of her signature designs is a reversible three-button silk jacket. She also offers light breezy tops with prints and embroidered patterns. World Piece has accessories as well, including scarves, and handmade jewelry. Ms. Grand can help you plan a trip to India, or she can take you there as a personal guide.

Danny's Jewelry & Watch Repair This dealer's cases are packed with platinum, gold, and silver estate jewelry, as well as an impressive collection of watches, and heaps of costume jewelry and accessories. Danny's also specializes in repairs of all kinds.

Frances Soukis Ms. Soukis presides over a table full of pretty things, including Fenton and other glass items, dainty teacups and lacy porcelain plates, and antique and vintage jewelry.

Feeling Hungry at the East 67th Street Market?

There is a fairly good selection of food, both prepared and fresh, at this market. The multiple vendors change from week to week, but in addition to Alexandra's Baked Goods and a vendor who sells mouthwatering Thai home cooking out of crockpots, you may also find:

Sara & Nancy's Farms There are several farmers represented at this market that offer fresh produce and flowers, including Sarah & Nancy's Amish farm stand, which also sells baked goods.

Bread Alone (www.breadalone.com) Bread Alone sells organic breads and baked treats at farmers markets all over the city. Choose among the fragrant and buttery brioche loaf, savory onion and olive focaccia, health loaf, rugelach, biscotti, and other sweet treats, all baked in the Catskills in a custom-designed cast-iron bread oven.

Pickles, Olives, Etc. (www.picklesandolives.com) If you're in the mood for a tart and crunchy snack, look for the wooden pickle barrels. In them, you'll find nine varieties of pickles, including kosher dills, full sours, hot full sours, cornichons, pickled peppers, and more. You can also find upwards of twenty varieties of olives, including Greek and oil-cured black olives and green olives stuffed with lemon, garlic, almonds, cheese, and peppers. In the "etcetera" category, you will find dried apricots, marinated mushrooms, sun-dried tomatoes, Turkish pistachios, and pepperoncini.

GreenFlea

Columbus Avenue (76th St. / 77th St.)
Sunday 10 am to 5:30 pm (November through March),
10 am to 6 pm (April through October);
see web site for Saturday hours during the holiday season
1 to 79th Street; B, C to 81st Street-Museum of Natural History
www.greenfleamarkets.com

The GreenFlea on Columbus Avenue is principally owned by the Parents' Associations of three neighborhood public schools and a portion of every sale goes to academic enrichment programs. Since the market was incorporated in 1985, more than $4 million has been contributed. The market takes place on Sundays in the playground, hallways, and cafeteria of P.S. 87. Five days a week, kids are eating peanut butter and jelly sandwiches on the lunchroom tables, but on Sunday, the same tables may display antique diamonds, Tiffany silver, and vintage cigarette lighters.

There are both outdoor and indoor sections, which makes GreenFlea a great destination year-round. The GreenFlea is one of the longest running flea markets in the city for good reason—the shopping is fantastic. I find myself astonished by the variety and quality of the goods I have come across there. The range of vendors and prices is vast, and the quality is consistent across the board. Like many of the other markets, it has a variety of traditional flea market vendors, as well as artisans and food purveyors. You will find everything from handmade chandeliers and furniture, to new and vintage clothing and housewares, to quality antiques and gold and platinum jewelry.

Long-term vendors occupy the same locations every weekend. You may meet the fellow with the vintage toasters, or the gentleman who invented Hush Puppies and now sells pristine vintage menswear. The vendors inside of the school sell primarily, but not exclusively, more traditional vintage and flea market items. Come here prepared to be surprised by what you may find, whether your budget is $10 or $10,000.

Outdoor Vendors

Bugged Out (www.bugged-out.com) Designer Dina Lerman's smiling bumblebees, worms, dragonflies, crickets, and other insects adorn adult and children's T-shirts, tote bags, and note cards. One of her new bestsellers is the cute brown "I Love New York" cockroach. You can find her collection of fruit and vegetable designs exclusively at the New York Botanical Garden shop and at the GreenFlea. Ms. Lerman donates a portion of the proceeds to MS Research at the MS Care Center of NYU Hospital for Joint Diseases. Look for Angelina Jolie carrying Bugged Out's ant totebag in the film "Salt."

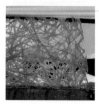

Luis da Cruz (www.luisdacruz.com) Luis da Cruz is a remarkable find at the GreenFlea. An architect by training, with years of experience working as a designer for Pierre Cardin, he is an interior designer who works in New York and Europe. He will custom-design and make architectural and whimsical curtains and other decorative items for your home, mixing industrial materials with ethereal fabrics.

Genuine Flea Market Guy—Larry Pinkus There are two types of flea-market shoppers. Some like to see organized booths, with items arranged by color, decade, function, or some other distinctive feature; others look at Pinkus's table piled high with stuff and think, "There's treasure in them thar hills!" If you are the latter, you will adore Larry's tables. Boxes of CDs, buckets of knickknacks, piles of teacups, statuettes, and spoons and maybe, just maybe, some real pearls in that tangled knot of shiny baubles.

Garden's Edge Antiques Based in Scituate, Rhode Island, Garden's Edge Antiques comes to the GreenFlea most weekends, bringing a good selection of rugs and furniture, all the right size for New York City apartments. Look for antique trunks and vintage tables, chairs, and shelves, as well as vintage glass. A portable martini bar with vintage highball glasses in emerald green was among recent items for sale, glinting glamorously in the Upper West Side sunshine.

Lightning Colors (www.lightningcolors.com) Find the chandelier of your dreams under this tent. Designer Ljatif Meqikukiq's sells both refurbished and custom-made fixtures using lead crystals from Germany, Spain, the Czech Republic, and Japan. You can also buy new and antique crystals in a large selection of shapes, colors, and sizes, to use in your own projects. You can pay retail prices at SoHo Treasures on Mercer Street—or purchase the chandeliers at the GreenFlea at a substantial discount. Pieces start around $150 and go up from there, depending on the size and details you desire.

Working Vintage Toasters (www.toastercentral.com)
Engineering marvels and objects of great beauty, the
1934 Toastmaster Pop-Up and the GE Spiderweb toasters offered here—along with other stunning vintage
specimens—are in perfect working order and come with
a guarantee. Owner Michael Sheafe knows pretty much
everything there is to know about toasters, and his collection is one of the highlights of the market. You can also find
other kitchen appliances from what Mr. Sheafe calls, "The
Golden Age of Chrome and Bakelite." Prices range from
around $40 to $500 for rare models such as the Sunbeam
Silent Automatic Toaster, circa 1938.

Wacky Magnets (www.wackymagnets.com) If you ever
played with a paper doll yourself, you remember how
frustrating it was to keep the clothes on using paper tabs.
Wacky Magnets has solved that problem. Owner Carolyn
Smith uses public domain images in her collections of
magnetic paper dolls of both children and animals. Her
motto is, "No batteries or remote control – just imagina-
tion!" Don't feel bad if you want to play with them yourself;
the first paper dolls were designed in the 1700s for adults.
Smith also sells humorous refrigerator magnets, including
Marilyn Monroe and Elvis drivers licenses, and a personal
favorite, "Beauty is in the Eye of the Beerholder."

Aunt Vicky's Bickys (www.auntvickysbickys.com)
Aunt Vicky's artisanal doggie biscuits are all natural and
baked without sugar, salt, or wheat. You may be tempted
to sample a banana pumpkin bar or a wheat-free sunflower
star yourself, but save it for the pup.

Off Broadway (www.boutiqueoffbroadway.com) Owned by a former Rockette, Off Broadway provides fine clothing and accessories aimed at female customers over forty. The clothing collections come from designers all over the world. Off Broadway also sells select vintage items. Another specialty is hats. "If you don't have a dog," quips proprietor Lynn Dell, "you must have a hat." For an even larger selection, walk down to the boutique at West 72nd Street and Broadway. Heidi Klum is a client of the flea market location; the store's clientele includes celebrities such as Kathleen Turner, Rita Moreno, and Phylicia Rashad.

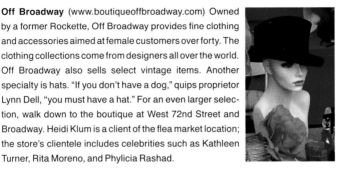

Indoor Vendors

Geno Sartori Vintage Cards Mr. Sartori has amassed a highly specialized and beautiful collection of vintage cards and other paper products, primarily unsold German stock, circa World War II, when the market for German goods disappeared. Sartori also sells elaborate pop-up cards and decoupage plates that he makes by hand, using the vintage images. It's difficult to walk by his table without something catching your eye, perhaps the dozen paper roses or the colorful vintage circus flyers.

Slope Antiques Susan and Richard Kurtzman present a shining array of silver plate antiques—trays, pitchers, tea sets, spoons, and more. Their items include antique Tiffany baby cups, as well as items from around the world. You may find a feminine Art Nouveau vase, or choose among a sweet collection of tea balls. They also have sterling silver personal items, such as brushes, mirrors, and, on one visit, a circa-1900 mesh handbag from Gorham Co. in pristine condition.

D. Flawless Inc. This antiques dealer offers European art and artifacts. You may find an original family crest from the House of Napoleon I, or a Bauhaus tea set from Napier. His beautiful porcelains may include a Dresden dog, Bohemian lamps, or delicate Royal Vienna candlesticks.

Rosalie Shostack Vintage Jewelry Hunt for overlooked gems on the $5 jumble table, or buy an antique lighter, pipe, or pen in mint condition. Search among trays and trays of jewelry, and boxes and boxes of vinyl records—treasures abound.

Feeling Hungry at the GreenFlea?

There are some wonderful food vendors at the GreenFlea. They change around each weekend, but you may find one or two of these options during your visit:

Yona's Delights (www.yonasdelights.com) Yona Amsalem makes wonderful bite-sized delights with a strong Lebanese and Greek influence, including hummus, spanakopita, baklava, and mushroom, vegetable, and spinach mini-quiches.

Baker Dan (www.bakerdan.com) Two words we all long to hear: healthy cookies. Afflicted with arthritis in his forties, Baker Dan began making tasty treats with natural ingredients. You can find gluten-free, sugar-free, lactose-free, and low-fat cookies, alongside the traditionally buttery, sugary standards such as chocolate chip and oatmeal.

Ma Mullen's Marshmallows Homemade marshmallows! They come in a wide variety of flavors, including peanut butter, chocolate, strawberry banana, grape, vanilla, cherry, and more. You can munch on them from a bag or eat them on a stick. The S'More's Kit, a basket filled with chocolate bars, graham crackers, and ample marshmallows, makes the perfect gift for your favorite chocoholic.

Hell's Kitchen Flea Market

West 39th Street (Ninth Ave. / Tenth Ave.)
Saturday & Sunday, 9 am to 6 pm
A, C, E, N, Q, R, 1, 2, 3, 7 to 42nd Street
www.hellskitchenfleamarket.com

Hell's Kitchen is the current location in the long and colorful history of one of the most exciting flea markets in the city. The market's heyday was in the late 1980s and 1990s when it was held on 26th Street and Sixth Avenue in Chelsea; at that location, it filled two large lots with six hundred vendors and more than 17,000 visitors each week. Celebrities, artists, models, dealers, tourists, and New Yorkers all flocked to the market every week in search of everything from large furniture items to costume jewelry. Stories abound of Andy Warhol and his entourage scouring the market for cookie jars and other kitschy collectibles.

As is the nature of markets, and of New York City itself, change was inevitable. The economic boom fostered a great deal of construction in Manhattan, and the empty lots where the markets were held became the sites of high-rise apartment buildings. The flea market found a new home in Hell's Kitchen on the far west side of Manhattan.

In a large lot near the Port Authority Bus Station and the West Side Rail Yards, you'll still hear the old-timers wax nostalgic about the old days in the Chelsea lots, but I'm here to tell you that there are loads of treasures to be found at the Hell's Kitchen location.

You can spend hours looking through the tables and racks at the market. If you are looking for vintage clothes and jewelry, the market has dealers selling carefully chosen items; many specialize in certain decades. This is where fancy shoes go to retire: Pradas, Ferragamos, and Jimmy Choos hang on the chain-link fences, ready for a polish and a new home. There is plenty of unique clothing for men as well. Furniture ranges from antiques to mid-century modern and later. Throwing a dinner party? Pick up a silver serving tray and crystal candlesticks here.

There are no food vendors at the Hell's Kitchen Flea. Fortunately, you are steps away from a wealth of dining options further up Ninth Avenue in the heart of Hell's Kitchen. Ask the vendors for recommendations, or simply venture uptown to find American diners and bakeries, as well as Italian, Japanese, French, and Turkish restaurants, and much more.

Kojo Volta Tribal Arts (www.hellskitchenfleamarket.com/vendors/kojovolta.php) Traditional African works of art abound at Kojo Volta's booth. This Sudanese dealer has a large variety of masks from all over Africa, especially from his own Dinka tribe. What really caught my eye were the hand-beaded belts. They're not only wearable, but also beautiful decorative pieces. Recently, one of his more unusual pieces was a beaded Dinka wedding corset, worn by both men and women, which would make quite a statement on a red carpet.

Diane's Treasures (www.hellskitchenfleamarket.com/vendors/diane.php) Everything old is new again at Diane Mioduzewski's booth. She has an impressive display of handbags, from a vintage Susan Gail Original clutch to a wide array of bags from the 1980s. Pick up a shiny Whiting & Davis mesh bag and join the ranks of Kim Cattrall and Renée Zellweger, who are fans of these classics. Mioduzewski also carries a large collection of "statement necklaces" that include huge pendants on thick metal chains. I spent a good hour reminiscing while going through her seventies painted flower pins and platform shoes; among the bright clothing, I noticed a pink and rust abstract 1980s Bob Mackie blouse for $20.

Store With No Walls (www.hellskitchenfleamarket.com/vendors/storewithnowalls.php) You'll find a jaw-dropping selection of vintage party dresses, suits, coats, shoes, hats, belts, and more—perhaps a vintage Chanel suit or a Christian Dior clutch—among the many racks and tables here. Items are priced to sell. Customers include actors and soap opera stars, as well as stylists from Broadway and cinema. Heidi Klum stops by regularly to see what's new. As Janet says, "We will always have something here for you, whether you're from Park Avenue or a park bench."

Ann's Corner
(www.hellskitchenfleamarket.com/vendors/annscorner.
php) Ann's tables are filled with stylish vintage and contemporary men's shoes in excellent condition. Score a
pair of Bally tassel loafers or some Cole Haan lace-ups,
or scour the rack of well-loved cowboy boots from $20.
In addition to footwear, she also has belts and ties to
complete any outfit.

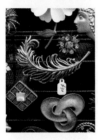

Karen & Rich Vintage The proprietors find most of their
objects at estate sales throughout the region. Cases and
tables overflow with jewelry, each piece—from a golden
feather brooch to a pearl pin—carefully tagged and displayed. You'll find handbags, too, ranging from vintage to
contemporary. Some of my favorite finds have been a hot
pink carry-on cosmetics case from the seventies, perfect
with the vintage shoulder bag emblazoned with the distinctive Pan American Airways logo.

The Bad Boys of 39th Street The two proprietors specialize in "things mechanical and musical." The first thing
you might notice is a gorgeous and fully functioning pho-
nograph glinting in the sun. They'll tell you it's their great-
great-grandfather's iPod and crank it up for you. Tables are
chock-full of wonderful things from mechanical toys to old
perfume bottles and tins full of skeleton keys.

Larry Finkel's Eclectic Junk Larry Finkel and his wife
have been selling at the flea market for many years. Their
tables are decorated with antique statuettes, sets of china,
vases, cordial sets, and vintage swizzle stick collections.
Old books, globes, and an elegant ice bucket are the perfect things for decorating a stately library.

Charles Adler Vintage Men's Clothing Charles Adler specializes in "the best of American vintage menswear, rugged work wear, and accessories." The collection, from the 1940s and earlier, includes some remarkable fashion artifacts. Designers from Armani, Ralph Lauren, and other fashion houses have purchased these high-quality vintage items for inspiration; Charles Adler supplies period clothing for movies and photo shoots as well. I was astounded by a 1930s jacket made of jute, which, despite the extremely fragile material, was in near-perfect condition ($500). These are valuable items and priced accordingly. Visits to the showroom in Greenwich Village are by appointment.

Old St. Patrick's Cathedral Market

Prince Street (Mulberry St. / Mott St.)
Monday to Friday 11 am to 7 pm, depending on the weather
B, D, F, V to Broadway-Lafayette Street; R, W to Prince Street; 6 to
Bleecker Street or Spring Street
www.oldcathedraloutdoormarket.com

Located between SoHo and Little Italy in Nolita (NOrth of LIttle ITAly), Old St. Patrick's Cathedral, the first cathedral built in New York more than two hundred years ago, still serves the neighborhood community. A small collection of vendors set up their tents in good weather, including these jewelry makers:

Shaya (www.shayanyc.com) The handmade sterling silver and gold-filled jewelry from Shay Mehubad is light, pretty, and geometric. His dynamic earrings, necklaces, rings, and bracelets composed of squares and rectangles draw customers from all over the country and the world.

Mano Jewelry Designs This artisan primarily makes rings for men and women using a combination of wood, sterling silver, and diamonds. Among the sumptuous exotic wood rings lined with silver is a remarkable design made of striated ebony with a small black diamond embedded in the wood.

Astrid Schumacher (www.astridschumacher.com) This former model and designer for Rubin Chapelle creates stylish handbags and yoga-inspired jewelry. The studded, lightweight "Hippie" bags and clutches are made from ultra-suede—perfect if you are looking for something unique, handmade, and animal-friendly. Schumacher's jewelry designs—including the 22-karat, vermeil Big Circle and Om necklace—are inspired by her travels in India and Indonesia.

Our Lady of Pompeii Crafts Market

Bleecker Street (Leroy St. / Carmine St.)
Saturday & Sunday, 11 am to 6 pm, April through December
A, B, C, D, E, F, V to West 4th Street

Located in the heart of Greenwich Village, the Pompeii Crafts Market first opened in 2001, scarcely a month after the attacks on the World Trade Center. The market maintains its positive and welcoming atmosphere.

Each weekend you will meet up to sixteen vendors, many of whom have been there since the beginning, set up on the sidewalk outside Our Lady of Pompeii, a Catholic Church and elementary school established in 1892 to serve a primarily Italian immigrant congregation.

The market features handmade hats, handbags, and other accessories. There are also vendors who sell vintage jewelry, as well as some who sell contemporary jewelry collections at excellent prices. One of the unique aspects of this market is that it is truly part of the neighborhood— many of the artisans live in the Village, within a few blocks of the market, and only sell their work here.

As you stroll down the sidewalk looking at all the handicrafts, you will rub shoulders with people from the neighborhood and tourists alike, all likely to be exploring, shopping, and eating at the specialty shops on Bleecker Street.

Fool's Gold Fool's Gold is the place to go for very special Bakelite jewelry. Proprietor Sheila Strong has many unique pieces to choose among, starting with a vintage cosmetics case loaded with bracelets in butterscotch, creamed corn, and other traditional Bakelite colors. The Bakelite cameos and hand-carved beaded necklaces are eye-catching, as is a hand-carved Art Deco bracelet—and its $675 price tag.

Le Primitive (www.leprimitivedesign.com) Two sisters from Rome make colorful necklace pendants of fused mosaic glass. Each piece is handcrafted in limited runs. Designs range from abstract shapes to hearts and flowers that are an unusual combination of sweet and edgy. The pendants are especially sensational in bright sunshine.

M & M Brazilian Jewelry This Brazilian mother and daughter design team works in a wide variety of styles, from chunky to delicate. Most of the designs are manufactured in Brazil, using native semi-precious stones. The daughter also makes a line of wrapped wire rings and earrings using crystals and brightly colored beads.

Monica Sigler Designs Designer and musician Monica Sigler combines natural and manufactured elements to create jewelry that has a spiritual aspect, with a fashionably industrial look. Pendants may be made with suede, feathers, pyrite, and geodes in combination with bolts, drill bits, tiny tiles, or Native American-style arrowheads.

Vintage Hats and Accessories Look for a big green umbrella; under it, you'll find this collection of vintage hats in straw, felt, or wool, all in perfect condition and beautifully made by fine craftspeople of yesteryear. You will also find vintage jewelry—mostly larger statement necklaces with pendants, pearls, and crystals.

Stacey Miller Unlimited

(www.staceymillerunlimited.com) Stacey Miller makes all her pieces by hand—cutting, hammering, and polishing or oxidizing each one to perfection. Or, she crochets them with silver or 14K-gold-filled wire. Both processes result in earrings, necklaces, and rings that are dainty yet make a bold statement. She works with sterling silver or 14K-gold backed with brass, and embellished with freshwater pearls, semi-precious stones, and Swarovski crystals. You may have seen Miller's designs worn by the hosts of "The View."

St. Anthony's Outdoor Market

South side of West Houston Street at Sullivan Street
Friday to Sunday 10:30 am to 6 pm
C, E to Spring Street; 1 to Houston Street
www.stanthonynyc.org/id6.html

Situated on the border of Greenwich Village and SoHo, the artisan market in front of St. Anthony's has been enlivening the sidewalk for more than twenty years. Many of the vendors change regularly, but some have been stationed on this stretch of sidewalk for quite a long time. Proceeds from the vendor fees go to support the Shrine Church of St. Anthony of Padua, which has been serving the community since 1866, when large numbers of Italian immigrants began coming to New York.

This is a relatively small market, but you can count on a good mix of vendors, from handmade jewelry to wonderfully colored slippers, as well as vintage clothes and soaps. There are also several young designers who sell their clothing at street markets in order to meet customers face-to-face and see the response to new designs. Some of the market's customers include neighborhood locals like Helen Hunt, Jesse Martin, Daryl Hannah, and Bebe Neuwirth. Although there are no regular food vendors, they occasionally show up; you may get lucky and come across one just when you are in dire need of a red velvet cupcake.

Drive Up To The Shades (www.driveuptotheshades.com) The sunglasses sold here are self-proclaimed "look-alikes," not knock-offs posing as the real thing. Designs are stylish and the prices excellent.

April May June Designs Designer April Clark makes practical and fun change purses and clutches, as well as leather headbands, by repurposing and recycling upholstery fabrics and leather.

Kimberlin Brown Jewelry (www.kimberlinbrownjewelry. com) Kimberlin Brown's style is youthful, and she looks to nature for inspiration. Her Black Forest Collection of earrings, necklaces, and rings consists of boxwood sprigs and laurel leaves cast in blackened silver and embellished with tiny black diamonds and a dewdrop-shaped moonstone. She also has a line based on bird and butterfly wings.

Dr. Bubbles Handmade Soap (www.drbubbles.artfire. com) Dr. Bubbles is a brand of 100% natural and vegetarian soap, handmade locally in small batches. These bars have no detergents, chemical additives, or preservatives, and they look and smell wonderful. Scents range from the relaxing bright purple Lovely Lavender to the luscious pick-me-up Vanilla Ylang Ylang.

AngelRox (www.angelrox.com) Clothing designer Roxi Suger has developed a versatile and flattering line of clothing. Among her smart designs are pull-on stretch jeans with a mesh waistband that makes them particularly comfortable. Her wings logos emblazon each back pocket, as well as her fun panties and tops. Another of her clever creations is The Wrap, a garment that can serve as a shirt, dress, skirt, shawl, or cape—perfect for travelers or people with typically tiny New York closets.

Sanuk Company This vendor first caught my eye because of the piles of colorful cloth slippers, designed and made by the Hmong tribe of Northern Thailand. The textiles and colors are beautiful, and the shoes themselves look stylish and are comfortable. Sanuk's owner, Jeremy Duffy, also designs jewelry and has the pieces made by craftspeople in Thailand. He makes larger pieces with tektites, black glass-like objects thought to be the result of meteors impacting the earth.

Young Designers Market

268 Mulberry Street (Prince St. / Spring St.)
Friday to Sunday, 11 am to 7 pm
6 to Spring Street; R, W, N to Prince Street;
B, D, F, V to Broadway-Lafayette Street
www.themarketnyc.com

The Young Designers Market is an important incubator in the New York fashion world. Founded in the fall of 2002, the market was originally inspired by the Henri Bendel concept of showcasing multiple new designers in one location, and is housed in the youth center gymnasium of the Old St. Patrick's Cathedral in Nolita—a humble location for the wealth of talent to be found there.

The designers sell handmade jewelry, hats, and a wide variety of handbags. There is women's and men's clothing, much of it avant-garde and creative yet wearable, as well as shoes, boots, and sandals. The best part is that you are buying these items directly from the designers themselves, most of whom create and produce the pieces right here in New York City. Prices are generally wholesale, which usually translates into a 40–60% discount off retail prices, sometimes more.

You will undoubtedly rub shoulders with New York's fashion trendsetters and trend spotters. Here, models, actors, stylists, and journalists get the jump on upcoming fashion designers and directions. Many, but by no means all, of the designers are unknown. You might see Tina Fey wearing a dress from Nature vs. Future, or catch a runway show of Tom Sohung's circle dresses at Fashion Week. Designers enjoy coming to this market because it allows them to talk with their customers and to learn what other designers are thinking about and working on.

Hundreds of shoppers visit the market each weekend. The summers are a great time to come to the market because most New Yorkers go out of town on the weekends. During November and December, there is a wonderful atmosphere for holiday shopping. If you want to send your favorite fashionistas over the moon, select their gifts at this market.

k* Shoes (www.kstar-nyc.com) Designer Keiko Hirosue's k* (pronounced "K-Star") designs are made for people (like New Yorkers, for instance) who want to look and feel good as they walk all over town every day; in other words, stylish yet comfortable. The Diva Thong is a stunning patent leather flat sandal that comes in coral and beige. You'll turn heads when you walk down the street wearing the k* gladiator sandal. Gabrielle Union is a regular client and Lily Allen picked up a pair of Glory Booties, suede ankle boots with a vividly colored silk lining, which she wore in a *Bust* magazine photo shoot.

Digby & Iona Jewelry (www.digbyandiona.com) Digby & Iona jewelry collections have a decidedly romantic eighteenth-century feel, yet the pieces are quite modern and edgy. Wanderer in a Sea of Fog is a gorgeous line of nautical-themed items, including a leggy octopus ring and the Lost Love Compass. The Hunter and the Hunted collection has a 14 Point Stag Ring and a Crossed Rifle Necklace. The iconic Inspector Closeau (sic) mustache necklace has been featured in *Nylon* magazine. Digby & Iona pieces can be found in shops in North America, Australia, and Europe.

Nature vs. Future (www.naturevsfuture.com) Clothing designer Nina Valenti launched her Nature vs. Future label in 2002. She creates her designs with the environment in mind, choosing organic, sustainable, renewable, and biodegradable materials, including organic cottons and wools, as well as fabrics made from seaweed and wood pulp. The garments, which sell in boutiques around the world, are notable for their sexy cutouts, edgy angles, and flattering shirring. The organic cotton Rebel Dress has been featured in Italian *Vogue*.

CLO Studio Lingerie (www.clostudio.com) Claudia Ochoa's sumptuous lingerie is delicate yet carefully engineered to provide support. This designer's collections are carried in more than one hundred boutiques in the U.S., including Luxe Lingerie in Beverly Hills, Peek A Boo in Aspen, and Coup de Foudre in Washington, D.C. She brings extra inventory from tradeshows to the Young Designers Market each weekend where you might just be lucky enough to pick up a one-of-a-kind piece.

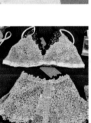

Charm NYC Hats (www.charmnyc.com) You can't be a hipster without the hat. Ume and Nicholas Taylor, designers and owners of Charm NYC, can help you find one. The classic Nicolini Fedora is unisex and a mainstay in any wardrobe. The retro Newsboy comes in a variety of patterns and fabrics, from houndstooth to pinstripe, and wool to linen. The saucy Three Buckle Beret and the charming Wild Rose are perfect for a chilly winter walk in the park.

Arza Handbag Design (www.arzadesign.com) Arza handbags combine beauty and function. They are handmade locally using soft Italian leather in both classic colors and metallics. The patented circular handle makes all of these bags—be it a wristlet, clutch, or a large shoulder bag—easy and comfortable to carry. The bags' rounded geometric shapes and pretty fabric linings make them recognizable as Arza originals. Arza's designs are carried in boutiques throughout the U.S., as well as in Ireland and Denmark.

Permanent and Semi-Permanent Markets
Brooklyn

Artists and Fleas

www.artistsandfleas.com

Locations:

Indoor Artists and Designers Market
129 North 6th Street (Berry St. / Bedford Ave.), Williamsburg
Saturday & Sunday, noon to 8 pm
L to Bedford Avenue, G to Metropolitan Avenue

Vintage Market
125 North 6th Street, Williamsburg, next door to
the Indoor Artists and Designers Market
Saturday & Sunday, noon to 8 pm
L to Bedford Avenue, G to Metropolitan Avenue

Market in McCarren Park
McCarren Park, adjacent to the McCarren Field House
in the northwest corner, Williamsburg
Saturday 10 am to 6 pm, May through September
L to Bedford Avenue, G to Nassau Avenue

The Artists and Fleas Market began in 2003 in a small, gutted commercial building off Bedford Avenue, the main street in Williamsburg, with space for just over thirty artisans. It has been growing ever since. A market dedicated to vintage items has recently opened next door, adding another twenty booths. The outdoor market launched in McCarren Park in 2009, with upwards of twenty vendors. This last market coincides with the Greenpoint Greenmarket on Saturdays. (p.237)

The market managers are careful to have a good mix of vendors selling a wide variety of handmade and vintage items. There are jewelry and accessory designers, as well as clothing and hat designers at both the indoor and outdoor markets. You can also find used books and vinyl records. The vintage market is filled with nostalgic items of past decades. Many of the artisans and designers sell their wares through well-known boutiques and retailers, but only here will you find their latest designs at direct-from-the-artist prices.

As with most of the markets, the group of vendors varies on any given day, but some of the vendors you may find at these markets include:

Indoor Artists and Designers Market

Georgia Varidakis Jewelry (www.georgiavaridakis.com) Georgia Varidakis acquires many of her eclectic charms and chains from retired jewelry makers and adds bits of watches and antique jewelry to make her delicate creations. She also makes tiny charms in silver and gold, on which she will hammer your initials while you wait.

Lynore Galore – Handmade Adornments

(www.1000markets.com/users/lynorestore) Trained as a master pearl stringer, Lynore Routte is a jewelry designer who makes wonderfully diverse pieces, not only for sale at the market, but for movies, photo shoots, and music videos. You may find her pieces in Bergdorf Goodman, as well. Look for her one-of-a-kind wide beaded bangles, round pendants made from vintage beads and crystals, and the distinctive silver leather fringe necklace.

Kreepy Doll Factory (www.kreepydollfactory.com)

Kreepy Doll maker Daniel Baxter is also producer, puppet designer, and co-writer on the Independent Film Channel's cooking show, *Food Party.* Among the wacky small dolls on Kreepy Doll Factory's tables you might see a teal blue guy with five legs and big green eyes, or one with a large round red head, a single eye and—unconventionally, for Baxter— only two arms. A creature named Argyle Bubbagum is the newest.

Dahlia Soleil Collection (www.dahliasoleil.com) Crocheting isn't just for grandmothers anymore. Paulette Jemmott-Wiley, owner of the Dahlia Soleil Collection, comes from a long line of crocheters. Among her funky and warm hats is a mustard yellow one with Wedgwood blue cameos on either side. Jemmott-Wiley also makes pretty T-shirts, appliquéd with her signature hummingbird, or a unicorn or big orange ant.

Gnome Enterprises (www.teeshirtgnome.etsy.com) Positioned at the elaborately designed booth just inside the front entrance to the market, Gnome sells T-shirts with funny, hip designs. Many of the designs depict the environment fighting back—look for Tree vs. Lumberjack and Squid Attacking Brooklyn Bridge.

Paigey (www.myspace.com/iampagey) Let illustrator Paigey make you into a sexy cartoon superhero or, better yet, villain. She sells her fun and saucy cartoon illustrations at Artists and Fleas, and you can commission her to do portraits. Paigey also makes necklaces featuring her characters.

Vintage Market

The Vintage Market is the place to go for vintage items, as well as vintage clothing that has been repurposed into new pieces. Located in the building next to the Indoor Market, the Vintage Market is housed in a former model loft apartment, so it has a less gritty feel than the indoor market.

The items being sold are almost always high quality and in good condition. Several vendors have private dressing areas where you can try on their clothing.

Jennifer Stewart Designs (www.jsdnyc.com) Jennifer Stewart is an expert seamstress who sews and sells repurposed vintage clothing. She will rework a vintage shirt, dress, or skirt and turn it into something unique and modern. She also makes new clothing out of vintage fabrics.

Lori's Loose Ends This dealer focuses on vintage clothing and accessories from the fifties, sixties, and seventies. She carries pieces by designers such as Bill Blass, Valentino, Gucci, and more—no surprise, since she says her sources are among the social elite of New York City. She has a talent for putting pieces together into wonderful ensembles, so ask for her advice.

Epoch Beads (www.epochbeads.etsy.com) Epoch Beads sells vintage jewelry supplies, including beads, chains, charms, and more and also offers custom jewelry design services in case you want something specific but do not want to make it yourself. It is great fun to look at all the different beads and findings from old jewelry, and to mix and match bits and bobs from different decades past.

The outdoor market at McCarren Park is conveniently located near the weekly farmers market nearby. There can be up to sixty vendors in the market.

Another Work In Progress

(www.anotherworkinprogress.com) The handmade notebooks, boxes, and picture frames by designer Dara Hymowitz combine nostalgia, utility, and fun. She acquires old favorite games like Monopoly, Scrabble, Clue—all the classics—and creates spiral-bound notebooks with covers made from the boxes. She also uses the spinners from vintage games like Twister and Limbo Legs to create wall clocks. She makes small jewelry boxes, too, as well as stationery and origami mobiles.

Umsteigen (www.iloveumsteigen.com)

Designer Susanne Schubert creates quirky and feminine casual clothes—T-shirts, hoodies, and dresses—each printed with graphic designs, all made and manufactured in Brooklyn. The jaunty blue-and-white-striped Loch Ness tee and hoodies printed with designs of bicycles, dinosaurs, and umbrellas manage to be sweet and urban at the same time. Umsteigen garments are sold in boutiques across the U.S. and Canada.

Alternative Art

(www.alternativeart.us) Alternative Art is a line of graphic T-shirts with silhouettes of trees, branches, and leaves silk-screened by hand onto soft, earth-toned garments.

Bullfrog Creatives (www.bullfrogcreatives.com) Rebecca Stern, owner of Bullfrog Studios, designs and makes a range of sculptural jewelry. Her signature Topography Locket looks like a tiny mountain, and flips open to store a memento or tiny love letter. Other pieces are made using a technique called "snow casting," by which molten silver is poured into snow to make unique organic shapes.

FusingColors (www.fusingcolors.com) The jewelry created by FusingColors is handmade from glass combined with oxides, stones, and other elements to create one-of-a-kind designs made in a studio in the Diamond District on 47th Street. There, the glass pieces are made and paired with leather to make comfortable rings, cuff bracelets, and necklaces.

Brooklyn Flea

Locations:

Ft. Greene Flea

Bishop Loughlin Memorial High School

176 Lafayette Ave. (Clermont Ave. / Vanderbilt Ave.), Ft. Greene

Saturday 10 am to 5 pm

C to Lafayette Avenue; G to Clinton-Washington Avenues;

2, 3, 4, 5, B, D, N, Q, R to Atlantic Avenue-Pacific Street

www.brooklynflea.com

Brooklyn Bridge Flea

Under the Brooklyn Bridge, at 22 Water Street

near corner of New Dock Street

Sunday 11am to 6pm

A, C to High Street; F to York Street; 2, 3 to Clark Street

www.brooklynflea.com

The outdoor markets run from April-November

(closed December-March)

Brooklyn Flea / Ft. Greene

Don't let the name confuse you—the Brooklyn Flea is much more than a traditional flea market. It hosts a wonderful mix of vendors selling handmade accessories, clothing, and art, and dealers of antiques, collectibles, salvaged architectural items and furniture, and more. There are currently two locations for the Brooklyn Flea, Ft. Greene

Bridge. Each market is written about separately because each offers distinct shopping and exploring experiences.

The Brooklyn Flea in Fort Greene—this is the original location—is held on the large playground of Bishop Loughlin Memorial High School. With a roster of over 150 vendors, the mix at the market changes every Sunday. Make sure you plan your visit around lunchtime because the food is remarkable. The food vendors are creative, fun, and local, and they sell delicious and unexpected kinds of food, both savory and sweet.

Although both locations close for the winter, many of the artisans and vendors can be found at the Gifted Holiday Market, sponsored by the Brooklyn Flea, from Thanksgiving weekend through Christmas Eve. (Check the website for location and hours.)

She Hit Pause Studios (www.shehitpausestudios. com) Photographer Matt Schwartz, owner of She Hit Pause Studios, creates vintage-looking images using a Polaroid camera. Anthropologie has sold his work in its home décor section. Look for his faded, evocative summertime images of Coney Island. Photographs range in price from $65–$200, depending on size and framing.

Focused Vintage (focusedvintage.blogspot.com) This vendor has thousands of wonderful old prints of all sizes and categories, as well as vintage photographic equipment. Mostly nostalgic scenes and formal portraits, there are some creepy photos, too, such as Victorian death images. Miss your old Kodak Brownie? Maybe you'll find another one here.

Osborn Design Studios (www.osborndesign.com) The colorful shoes here are handmade in Guatemala by cobblers and tailors using fabrics made by its indigenous people. The slip-ons, lace-ups, and ankle boots are designed by Osborn Studios, who oversee the production and bring them to the market. These shoes can also be found in several boutiques in New York City, including Oak in Manhattan and Alter in Greenpoint.

Alison Tauber (www.alisontauber.com) Textile designer Alison Tauber makes clothing and household items. She sells organic cotton T-shirts and scarves with stylized flower, seed pod, and butterfly designs, as well as pincushions, throw pillows, blank books, and more.

Loyalty and Blood (www.loyaltyandblood.com) David Denosowicz and Maggie Doyle, owners of Loyalty and Blood, sell handmade jewelry, clothing, and tote bags. If you need a funky tote bag for your groceries, consider the Lucha Libre mask or atomic mushroom cloud designs. The jewelry is mostly made with brass charms, including hearts, keys, wrenches, bows, balloons, Eiffel Towers, flowers, birds, and peace signs. Loyalty and Blood sells designs at Urban Outfitters throughout the U.S. and at the Therapy boutiques in California.

Olde Good Things (www.oldegoodthings.com) For antique and vintage home décor items, stop by and see the "architecturologists" at Olde Good Things. The items change weekly, but mirrors and picture frames made from antique tin ceiling panels are always available, as is furniture made from reclaimed wood. There are Olde Good Things stores in New York, New Jersey, and Los Angeles.

Feeling Hungry at the Brooklyn Flea / Ft. Greene?

Food options at the Flea are many and mouthwatering. There are approximately twenty-five food vendors; you may find some of the following each weekend:

Kumquat Cupcakery (www.kumquatcupcakery.com) Owner, Williamsburg resident,and graduate of the French Culinary Institute Keavy Landreth specializes in bite-sized mini-cupcakes in scrumptious and unusual flavors. The peanut butter ones are a cakey version of a peanut butter cup, and the red velvet are a mouthful of just-sweet-enough goodness. Kumquat's mini-cupcakes taste fresh from the oven of a happy Brooklyn kitchen—and they are.

Pizza Moto Brooklyn (www.pizzamotobklyn.com) Brick oven pizza at the flea market? Pizza Moto pulls it off using a mobile brick oven. Seriously—wood, fire, and all, is carted all around town, producing hot and fragrant pizzas that use Aiello's Mozzarella from Brooklyn and wild oregano from Sicily. Pizza Moto also caters.

Asia Dog (www.asiadognyc.com) Forget mustard and ketchup. Asia Dog sells hot dogs and burgers with Asian-inspired toppings, including Japanese curry and homemade kimchi apples, Asian sesame slaw, seaweed flakes, and more. Each week a different mix of toppings is featured.

Blue Marble Ice Cream (www.bluemarbleicecream.com) Blue Marble sells its ice cream— made from local and fair trade ingredients—from an ice cream tricycle. Purists will love the vanilla, chocolate, and coffee flavors; the more adventurous may be tempted by pumpkin and maple.

Whimsy & Spice (www.whimsyandspice.com) Whimsy & Spice sells cookies, biscotti, and marshmallows, all made by hand in Brooklyn. Unusual delicacies include hazelnut chocolate whisky sandwich cookies, perfect with a cup of coffee, and Earl Grey sandwich cookies, perfect with a cup of tea.

The Brooklyn Flea opened this second outpost in the summer of 2009 just under the Brooklyn Bridge in the neighborhood known as DUMBO ("Down Under the Manhattan Bridge Overpass"). The views of the Brooklyn and Manhattan bridges and Manhattan are breathtaking in this former industrial area that was first settled by artists in the mid-1980s and nineties and now is home to many young families. When you get off the subway, ask anyone for directions either to the flea market or the bridge. You can't really miss either.

There are more than one hundred merchandise and food vendors at this market. It is easy to make a day out of visiting this destination, beginning or ending with a walk over the Brooklyn Bridge. After you have exhausted your resources at the market, there is a beautiful park between the Brooklyn and Manhattan bridges with lots of green space, a playground, and a small beach where people skip stones or bring their dogs for a swim. A stroll up nearby Water Street will lead you to Jane's Carousel, painstakingly hand restored "for the children of New York" by artist Jane Walentas. See the website janescarousel.com for the announcement of the permanent move to Brooklyn Bridge Park.

While many of the same vendors from the Saturday market in Ft. Greene go to this market on Sundays, the overall feeling and clientele are slightly different. While Ft. Greene market has a distinctly neighborhood feel, the DUMBO market is more of a destination. As with the Ft. Greene market, the vendors at the DUMBO market often rotate, so it is worth coming back several times to see the entire variety of merchandise offered.

Long-established vendors and an ongoing crop of new artists

and entrepreneurs keep this market dynamic and vibrant—and full of great stuff.

Birdhouse Jewelry (www.birdhousejewelry.com) Amy and Alan Lapierre create unusual pieces, necklaces with pendants of glass and semi-precious stones, with unexpected accents—perhaps their signature small bird charm or a DJ's headset—incorporated into the chain. They make rings and earrings, too.

R. Bernard Estate Liquidators R. Bernard Butler comes to the Brooklyn Flea several times a month from Washington, D.C., bringing vintage furniture and decorative items as well as jewelry. If you're looking to furnish your apartment with conversation pieces at great prices, Bernard is the person to talk with—and he just might sell you a pink plush sofa.

Grace Napoleon Handmade Clothes and Collectibles (www.etsy.com/shop/gracenapoleon) Grace Napoleon has created a collection of decorative items with a distinct 1950s feel. She also makes "clothes from clothes"; in other words, she takes used clothing, cuts it up, and sews the pieces back together differently, remaking styles and patterns, using contrasting thread, and adding details. Each piece is one-of-a-kind, cute, and hip.

Hideya Sagawa's Vintage American West This avid collector from Japan has a talent for finding rare and unusual vintage items from the American West. He has a variety of traditional and unusual cowboy boots, but his collections of belts and jewelry are the most interesting: you might find an old pouch made from a turtle shell, or a shaman's leather bag filled with mysterious objects.

The New New NY (www.thenewnewny.com) The New New NY is an artists' cooperative in the city that brings different artists to the Brooklyn Flea each week. Martin Lopez (www.adornmentsnyc.com) makes new jewelry out of vintage beads and findings. Andrea and Juan Arango of Caja Jewelry (www.cajajewelry.com) create edgy silver charms, such as anatomically correct hearts and lungs, and custom nameplates à la Carrie Bradshaw. Anne Arden McDonald (www.anneardenmcdonald.com) makes silver castings of items such as tiny plant roots, apple seeds, and Victorian lace.

Australian Scent (www.australianscent.com) Megan and Eddie Enriquez have created a line of skincare products that includes chemical-free moisturizers, scrubs, hair products, and more, all displayed in a booth that looks like a spa in a rainforest.

Brooklyn Brew Shop (www.brooklynbrewshop.com) The brainchild of Erica Shea and Stephen Valand, the Brooklyn Brew Shop sells beer-making kits fit for a New York apartment—the kits take up less than one square foot of space. Buy a gallon brew bottle, air lock, plastic tubing, and pre-mixed ingredients. Flavors vary by season and whim; try the grapefruit honey ale or the chocolate maple porter.

Kelsi Vintage 60s and 70s Kelsi sells groovy clothes—most of the pieces unworn old samples and dead stock from the sixties and seventies—at good prices. Get tricked out in a new denim jumpsuit from 1974 and boogie down.

Feeling Hungry at the Brooklyn Flea / Brooklyn Bridge?

There are many wonderful local and artisanal food vendors at the market who alternate each weekend. Here are some you may find:

Red Hook Lobster Pound (www.redhooklobsterpound.com) Get in line early for one of the yummy Maine lobster rolls from this Brooklyn-based company—they sell out quickly.

People's Pops (www.peoplespops.blogspot.com) Three Brooklyn-based partners use fresh, organic fruits and herbs from local farmers markets to make popsicles in flavors such as peaches and cream, sour cherry and sweet strawberry, lemon and ginger, and—my favorite—blueberry and cardamom. The flavors depend on what ingredients are in the greenmarkets, so the variety is endlessly changing, and delicious.

Red Hook Food Vendors (www.myspace.com/redhookfoodvendors) This group of "artisan cooks" sells Latin American food. The Salvadoran pupusas (cheese or sausage-filled tortillas), are flavorful and authentic; the Mexican tacos and flautas hot and spicy.

LuxSugar (www.lux-sugar.com) For a sweet snack stop by Lux Sugar. The baked goods, named after celebrities, include mini-cupcakes called the Marilyn Monroe (red velvet), the Perez Hilton (strawberry), the Prince Harry (carrot), the George C (dreamsicle), and the Samantha (lemon with lemon vodka–infused icing).

Liddabit Sweets (www.liddabitsweets.com) Liddabit Sweets makes caramels, jellies, chocolate bars, lollipops, and more from local seasonal ingredients. You'll find locally brewed beer in both the pretzel caramels and the Slurtle, a traditional turtle made with the beer caramel.

Brooklyn Indie Market

Smith and Union Streets, Carroll Gardens
Saturday 11 am to 7 pm, Sunday 11 am to 6 pm;
April through December
F, G to Carroll Street
www.brooklynindiemarket.com

The Brooklyn Indie is a little jewel of a market that first opened its doors—or, more accurately, its tent flaps—in 2006. Committed to promoting craftsmanship, the market is home to up to twenty vendors on each day, a mix of several permanent vendors and some who rotate every weekend. The market itself is steps away from the Carroll Street subway station and the weekly neighborhood greenmarket.

The Indie is right in the center of Carroll Gardens, now a bucolic Italian and Irish neighborhood in Brooklyn near the Gowanus Canal. You will see old Italian couples strolling down the sidewalk, alongside the newer arrivals, who are young families and hipsters alike. You will see baby strollers during the day and lots of people out enjoying themselves in the neighborhood at night.

One of the most unusual aspects of the Brooklyn Indie Market is its annual Steampunk Day. Usually held in October the week before Halloween, this fashion show attracts hundreds of Steampunkers and spectators, so get there early. For the uninitiated, Steampunk is a sub-culture built around what might be described as retro-futuristic design. Steampunkers dress in a mix of Victorian-era styles combined with Goth and a touch of Mad Scientist. Think, "Jules Verne meets Johnny Rotten."

The Indie Market usually does not have food vendors, but not to worry. The neighborhood has many good restaurants and coffee shops, and it has become known as a mecca for brunch. When you come to the market, plan on spending some time exploring the neighborhood and trying some of the traditional Italian restaurants or the international and American eateries.

Fofolle Designs (www.fofolle.com) Designer Kathy Malone, who is also a co-founder and manager of the Brooklyn Indie, designs and sews innovative and feminine clothing. One of her most sought-after items is the multi-use skirt/poncho. Yes, you can wear it as a flattering asymmetrical skirt or pop it over your shoulders as a stylish slouch-neck poncho. Fofolle makes these garments in summer- and winter-weight fabrics in many colors and patterns. Kathy also "reinvents" vintage clothing by snipping, sewing, and adding new buttons and ribbons. She can turn an unflattering seventies boxy brown velvet blazer into a smart, form-fitting jacket.

Knit Knit (www.etsy.com/shop/knitknit) Artist and designer Nguyen Le knits witty and whimsical pea pods and leaves to make pins and earrings, and uses felting techniques to create woolen cameo pendants with silhouettes of bunnies, whales, and girls with ponytails, and—my favorite—commas and semicolons. Her knit "power cord" can be used as a skinny scarf, decorative belt, or curtain tie. She recently sent a cable knit postcard to Martha Stewart through the mail with the message, "Wish I was there." Shortly thereafter, she appeared on the show.

Off The Mat (www.offthemat.be) Off The Mat is a line of natural yoga-inspired products. The deeply scented soaps, oils, candles, and shea butters come in several collections. The 7 Chakras Collection includes Anja (herbal, warm vanilla notes) and Muladhara (floral, musk, violet notes). The Black Collection is a series of botanical balms and sprays. Every product uses natural and vegan ingredients. Yoga clothing and bags and jewelry made from rubber yoga mats round out the collection.

Tracey Toole (www.traceytoole.com) Seamstress Tracey Toole started making bags more than ten years ago. She's still sewing, now using vintage and vintage-inspired fabrics to make totes, aprons, napkins, throws, pet beds, and pretty much everything you'd need to make your house a home. Her striped and appliquéd tea towels and napkin sets are dainty and useful. Your kitty will appreciate the fuzzy cat bed with organic catnip sewn into it.

Wonder Threads (www.wonderthreads.com) Need more ridiculously cute clothes for your children or for your own inner child? Wonder Threads' designs sport images hand-appliquéd onto onesies, tiny tees for the kids, and bigger tees for adults. Check out the owl, squirrel, ladybugs, strawberries, dinosaurs, and mushrooms. I am partial to the nostalgic designs, like the bright Big Wheels in primary colors and the seventies-style unicorn.

Huggy Bunny (www.huggybunny.com) Not only do Huggy Bunny's kids clothes have delightful graphics, they are also made from a type of 100% pima cotton developed by the designer's father. Babies will feel cozy in footie pajamas covered with light yellow bunnies and bright orange carrots. T-shirts with two green frogs sitting on lily pads are cute on both boys and girls. Hummingbirds flutter around pink daisies on a toddler's dress.

Rocks and Salt (www.rocksandsaltdesign.com) Rocks and Salt creates limited-edition handmade hats for all seasons. For summer, the funky Carmelita bucket hat is perfect for a day out shopping or sitting at the beach. For winter and fall, the Amelia is a timeless woolen aviator cap with a chinstrap that would have been as stylish in the thirties as it is today. The small-brimmed Lola comes with earflaps that can be worn down or snapped up. The Henley is a cotton topper with three quirky bowling pins toppling over. Almost a turban, the Rita with her jaunty ruching comes in rich cashmere for the cold and cotton jersey for the warmer months.

Lulu S. Soap Co. (www.lulussoapco.com) Lulu S.'s table is a jumble of good-smelling and beautifully colored hand-made soaps. Made from coconut oil, olive oil, palm oil, and castor oil, they come in a wide array of delectable scents like "pumpkin brûlée," "oatmeal milk honey," "bourbon de vanille," "Marrakesh," "grass stain," and "Havana nights." Owner Michele Maldonado Milner started making soaps in order to have something fun to do with her now-teenage son. She says the soaps are "tested only on teenagers"— rest assured that they are her own sweet-smelling brood.

The Makers Market at the Old American Can Factory

232 Third Street at Third Avenue, Gowanus
Sunday (check website for updated hours)
F, G to Carroll Street; F, G, M, and R to Fourth Avenue-Ninth Street
www.thecanfactorymarket.org

This market, which started in 2009, has consistently had some of the highest quality handmade goods and artisanal foods that I have come across. Thoroughly curated by the organizers, the market itself takes place in one of the large garage bays of the former factory, so it is indoors and quite beautiful in an industrial way.

The Old American Can Factory itself is worth coming to see. Built between 1865 and 1901, this 130,000-square-foot building has been converted into studio spaces for more than two hundred artists, designers, filmmakers, publishers, performers, and nonprofit organizations, many of whom you will meet at the market. The Can Factory also hosts Rooftop Films, screening movies and short films throughout the summer, as well as concerts in the Courtyard and the Garage. It is worth sticking around after the market for one of these local events.

This is a true "makers market," where you cannot only purchase directly from the people who make the items, but you can also see some of the artisans at work. You may see an old letterpress producing beautiful note cards, or a leather craftsman stitching together a bicycle bag. The mix of artisans, music, and food make you want to linger, talk with the artisans, and take home some beautiful finds.

The types of things you will find at this market will vary, and each weekend offers up new discoveries. All of the participants are local and represent the vibrant creative community of the Factory. In order to sell at this market, they must meet well-defined criteria around "quality, integrity, and accountability of production." Shoppers will find beautiful, unique, and high-quality products here, and the satisfaction of supporting the people who make them.

Parable Ink (www.parableink.com) Parable Ink designs and prints a variety of stylish tees for men and women and one-size-fits-most dresses. The images make you think, or at least wonder about them; they tell a story—a parable, if you will. One shirt has an image of a boy fishing that looks like it came straight from a Grecian urn in the Met. Another is a traditional Indonesian mask with its tongue sticking out. Parable Ink is also the original designer of the now ubiquitous orange "Parking Ticket" T-shirt, which tells its own distinctly New York story.

Nancy Nicholson Stained Glass (www.nancy-nicholson.com) Nancy Nicholson's stained glass isn't the type of stained glass you'll see in European cathedrals, although she uses similar traditional methods to create her work. Her images are photo-realistic and enhanced by the richly colored glass and the light that streams through them. I'm drawn to the silhouetted tree series, but I am also partial to her cityscapes of classic New York water towers, the Brooklyn Bridge, or a construction site.

Kataplin (www.kataplin.com) Kataplin's T-shirt designs are mostly geared towards funky babies and cool kids, but adults can wear them too. The designs themselves may be simple stick-like drawings of ants and aliens, or a big print of a shark with lots of teeth, but they all have a humorous and urban edge to them. Perro in NYC is a funny triangular black dog standing on the Brooklyn Bridge with the city skyline behind it. Kataplin also has a line of colorful children's slippers that look very comfy for tiny feet.

Christine Vasan Jewelry (www.christinevasan.com)
You can see and feel the influence of nature on Christine
Vasan's delicate jewelry designs, as well as her lovely
displays. Her Anise collection is based on the star anise
pod, a form that is artistically represented in silver and gold
with white sapphires. Vasan makes a beautifully simple
necklace of silver-cast keishi pearls strung on a chain of
crocheted silk thread as well as wedding rings in platinum
or gold with precious stones. She will also make custom
pieces to order.

Atelier Leather Goods (www.mosatelier.blogspot.com)
Marc Schreiner grew up around saddle makers and now
uses Old World techniques to make men's satchels, ladies'
handbags, and accessories. He cures leather in vegetable
dyes made from tree bark and hand finishes the pelts to
ensure the rich hues and a buttery texture. He often incor-
porates carved hardwood bases into his designs that allow
him to create bags in unusual shapes, such as a teardrop.

ERL Creations (www.analoged.etsy.com) Ed Ledner is
a retired engineer who now devotes his time to learning
new jewelry-making techniques, the results of which are
on display at the factory. His folded cuff bracelets have a
natural patina that gives depth and form to a single sheet
of copper. Using a process called Kum-boo, Mr. Ledner
embeds molten gold onto textured silver domed earrings
for a bi-colored effect.

May Luk Ceramics (www.takemehomeware.com) Trained at Glasgow School of Arts, May Luk designs plates, bowls, and platters with a hint of Victorian mixed with a touch of iPod. You may have to look twice to confirm what you are seeing in her designs. One plate features the silhouette of a squirrel with a top hat. Don't miss her Brooklyn Chinoiserie china, decorated with a water tower, Manhattan Bridge, and other borough icons. May Luk also takes custom orders for Bespoke Cameo Ware, featuring your very own patrician profile on a bowl or plate.

Meow Meow Tweet (www.meowmeowtweet.com) This Brooklyn-based design team's hand-drawn labels are almost as much fun as the soaps they wrap—one might expect as much from a company called Meow Meow Tweet. The high-quality soaps made with organic bases and essential oils include Citronella Fir, a favorite among campers (a drawing of Sasquatch adorns the label). One of my favorites is Black Tea Honey, made with Assam black tea.

WarpeDesign

(www.warpedesign.etsy.com) The lampshades, tea light covers, and greeting cards from WarpeDesign are created using a technique known as Pin Art, in which paper is pierced with multiple pinholes to form a design and an embossed texture. Light shining through the holes creates an illuminated piece of practical art. WarpeDesign's String Theory pattern looks like "Mardi Gras beads thrown into the air," while Grey Scales casts a series of light patterns on any nearby wall.

Hungry at the Old American Can Factory?

Take advantage of food from the artisanal cooks, bakers, and chocolatiers at the market. Vendors change from week to week, but you can always find healthy and delicious fare—and even a beer—here.

SchoolHouse Kitchen (www.schoolhousekitchen.com) SchoolHouse Kitchen creates and sells mustards, dressings, marinades, and chutneys. The two types of mustards offered, Sweet Smooth Hot and Horseradish Dill, are not only used as condiments but for rubs and roasting as well. The orange and chili Squadrilla Chutney packs quite a flavor punch. The kitchen makes some classic dressings and marinades, too, such as Balsamic Vinaigrette Basico and Ginger Lime Vinaigrette.

Hot Bread Kitchen (www.hotbreadkitchen.org) Hot Bread Kitchen teaches immigrant women bread-making to help them ensure their economic wellbeing. The Hot Bread Kitchen line of breads is made from locally grown, organic ingredients whenever possible. One of the best-selling products is hand-ground tortillas made from red, white, and blue Mexican corn, a specialty inspired by the home region of many of the bakers. Other products include crispy lavash crackers and focaccia buns, alongside the traditional European style baguettes and loaves and My Mom's Nutty Granola.

Nunu Chocolates (www.nunuchocolates.com) These rich and creamy confections are handmade in Brooklyn from single origin chocolate grown on a family farm in Colombia. Nunu is known for its soft caramels and ganaches. The hand-dipped salt caramels are buttery sweet with a crunch of savory salt. The raspberry ganache uses organic fruit puree made in Nunu's kitchen. The chocolates have been mentioned in *Gourmet*, *The New York Times*, *New York*, and *Modern Bride*, and on many food blogs.

Meeker Avenue Flea Market

391 Leonard Street (at Meeker Ave.), Williamsburg
Thursday to Sunday, 11 am to 7 pm
G to Metropolitan Avenue, L to Lorimer Street
www.meekeravenuefleamarket.com

The Meeker Avenue Flea Market is one of the newest entries onto the scene. A huge effort is being made to launch it in a fun and dynamic way. The number of vendors increases each week, and there is plenty of room to expand. The facility itself—an old manufacturing warehouse where clothing used to be processed and packaged for sale overseas—is perfect for a year-round flea market. This industrial history is apparent in the vibe of the market, but the building has been cleared out, spiffed up, and the interior painted a bright and cheery yellow. The plan is to add heating and air conditioning to make it a comfortable place to browse and shop in all weather. There are plans to add a coffee shop selling locally made sweets.

The market already has a nice balance of vendors selling new, vintage, and handmade items. I have found handmade jewelry and Indian and Tibetan artifacts; there is also a great T-shirt designer, Wear U From, with some typically Brooklyn-esque designs. One of my favorite vendors is a young fellow from the neighborhood who brings things from his overflowing apartment to the market. He sets up his booth to look like a living room, where he sells books, handmade furniture, piles of dusty chandelier crystals, and more. Frequent events and offers lure and entertain shoppers, including live music, a DJ, or karaoke.

Park Slope Flea Market

180 Seventh Avenue (1st St. / 2nd St.), Park Slope
Saturday & Sunday, 9 am to 5 pm
F to Seventh Avenue
www.parkslopefleamarket.com

The Park Slope Flea Market, a neighborhood fixture for more than thirty years, is held in the schoolyard of Public School 321; the vendors' fees go to support the school's academic activities. With a roster of five hundred vendors, there are approximately fifty vendors at this outdoor market every Saturday and Sunday, year-round, rain or shine.

The market has a laid-back vibe, much like the neighborhood itself. Located alongside Prospect Park, Park Slope is a beautiful old neighborhood filled with classic brownstones.

You can get the lay of the land fairly quickly, but take your time to browse slowly through the market because there is a lot there to see. It has a good mix of used books and collectibles, antique furniture, vintage clothing, and more. The first time I went, I took a cursory overview of the place in fifteen minutes; the next time I stayed for four hours.

I have known vendors to bring special items to the market upon request. If you are looking for something in particular, it is worth talking to them about what you want. Quite possibly, they have what you are looking for. If it's not with them at the market, they will be happy to bring it for you to look at next week.

Treasured Books Vendor Leanne Greenseid sells rare and first editions and children's books. The books she brings to the market are mostly contemporary used books, but she is an excellent resource for more valuable volumes, which you can see by appointment.

Chastiques The collection of tiny things on Chastiques' table caught my eye as I walked by. Among the many items was a 1950s pixie (faded everywhere except his smile), minute pewter Vikings, a porcelain stork carrying a smiling baby, a stack of old photographs, Domino Sugar canisters, porcelain figures, vintage glass bottles, and a fun old snow globe for your desk.

Grandma's Attic Furniture Grandma's Attic sets up mid-century modern furniture and accessories in attractive vignettes to showcase the entire collection. The "kitchen" might feature a highly collectible 1950s chrome table and chairs in mint condition. In the "living room" display a hot pink armchair with nubby upholstery might be placed next to a record player console and a blond coffee table adorned with a vintage martini set.

Shazzy's Vintage Classics Each item sitting on Shazzy's table and hanging on the clothing rack is carefully selected and displayed, so it is easy to find the treasures here. Handbags are in excellent condition—you might be enticed by a vintage Fendi or a 1930s alligator bag. One weekend, a pair of jaunty brown and white Prada shoes sat next to a brown suede and tweed fedora. Try on a few possibilities and check yourself out in Shazzy's signature gold-framed mirror.

Bonsai by Raymond Tam Mr. Tam is a Bonsai artist. His miniature trees take years to grow and are cultivated limb-by-limb, leaf-by-leaf. Mr. Tam creates diminutive Tea Trees, Japanese Elms, Chinese Elms, and several other varieties; he also provides instructions on how to keep yours thriving. If you are in the process of killing your own Bonsai, Mr. Tam will revitalize it for you. Bonsais are the perfect size for New York apartments. These living works of art are $30–$50.

Marly Malone at The Hand Laundry (www.marlymalone.com) Marly Malone's Brooklyn brownstone home was a real hand laundry years ago, and she named her online and flea market shops after this bit of history. She takes iconic images of Brooklyn, some her own drawings, and has regional artisans turn them into jewelry, tea towels, paperweights, and sun-catchers. Malone also sells Irish and Scottish jewelry and keepsakes such as Claddagh rings and Celtic knots, as well as beautiful linen children's clothing—but you'll have to launder them yourself.

West African Designs
(www.internationaleducationalservices.com) You can't miss the bright African batik fabrics hanging along the back wall of the schoolyard, which have been made into beautiful and practical items such as aprons, belts, bags, and fragrant sachets. The fabric is hand-designed, and each item is hand-sewn by Dr. Natalie Gray, Director of International Educational Services, an organization that serves subsistence farmers in Ghana. Proceeds from the sale of these items go to support this fourteen-year-old small non-profit organization.

Annual and Semi-Annual Markets
Manhattan

American Crafts Festival

Lincoln Center (Columbus Ave. at W. 64th St.)
Generally the second and third weekends in June
(check website for details)
1 to 66th Street-Lincoln Center
www.craftsatlincoln.org

This annual event, presented by the American Concern for Art and Craftsmanship (ACAC) draws well over two hundred artisans from around the country. It is held annually on the grounds of Lincoln Center for the Performing Arts on the Upper West Side of Manhattan. You can't miss the white tents set up alongside the iconic white buildings of Lincoln Center.

There are all types of arts and crafts at all price ranges—jewelry, blown glass, paintings, sculpture, handmade clothing, leather goods, and wooden crafts.

During the day there are musical performances, and food vendors are sprinkled in among the crafters, selling crepes, popcorn, watermelon, and other tasty foods that are easy to eat while you stroll through the tents.

The setting is beautiful and the quality of the crafts is high. There are hundreds of artisans at this craft fair; I am highlighting a select few whose work is representative of quality craftsmanship:

Meb's Kitchenwares (www.mebskitchenwares.com)
Meb Boden and Tom Vaiciulis make wooden spoons, salad sets, pie servers, cutting boards, and drawer handles— including pieces specifically designed for lefties and children. If you're looking for a cutting board with the silhouette of a Labrador retriever inlayed in darker brown wood, you'll find it here. One spoon they make has a whale's tail handle, others are based on those used at Shinto shrines. The artisans use only woods harvested in New England, including some from their own Connecticut backyard.

Cindy Avroch Studios (www.cindyavrochstudios.com): The sheer variety of decorative items from Cindy Avroch Studios lured me into her tent. Using the technique of decoupage, Ms. Avroch creates gorgeous French country platters, Victorian insect paperweights, architectural lamps, and much more. Her work has been featured in many magazines, and she makes all of her creations in her New York studio.

Natures Creations Natural Jewelry and Art
(www.leafpin.com) Artist Dennis Ray creates leaf jewelry in all sizes, colors, and finishes. Because each leaf is a real leaf, covered in copper and finished with other metals or a patina for different effects, each has a unique special shape and imperfections. When I picked up an oak leaf with an acorn attached, I could hear the actual acorn rattling around inside the copper shell. If you have a special tree of your own, Natures Creations will create custom pieces using its leaves.

Jan Huling – Beadist (www.janhuling.com) Jan Huling's work is somewhat reminiscent of intricate Zulu beadwork, but rather than making adornments, she applies beads to other objects to create new works of art. One recent work of hers was a fearsome large jackal doll covered in beadwork patterns. Huling also beads brightly striped cats, birds, and dancing crickets, as well as business card holders and pillboxes. The most spectacular piece she displayed at a recent fair was a child's toy grand piano decorated with vivid paisleys of colored beads, and inlaid with gems and medallions.

Broadway Cares/Equity Fights
AIDS Flea Market

Shubert Alley at West 44th Street (Broadway / Eighth Ave.)
Annually in September (check website for dates)
1, 2, 3, 7, A, C, E to 42nd Street
www.broadwaycares.org

Broadway Cares/Equity Fights AIDS (BC/EFA) "draws upon the talents, resources, and generosity" of the Broadway community to raise money (so far, more than $160 million) for AIDS-related causes in the U.S. The organization holds several spectacular fundraising events each year, including the Easter Bonnet Competition and Broadway Bares, a variety show with performers from all the major Broadway shows. Tickets to these events are coveted items. One wonderful event that is accessible to all, however, is the annual Flea Market and Grand Auction.

Broadway fans from around the world plan their visits to New York City around the BC/EFA Flea Market and Auction, and for good reason. There is nothing quite like it in the city, or possibly the world. Imagine all the big Broadway theaters clearing out their closets, and selling the wonderful and unusual items for affordable prices right in Times Square. That is exactly what happens every year in Shubert Alley and on 44th Street.

In 1987, at the height of the AIDS epidemic, the cast and crew of *A Chorus Line* decided to raise money for the cause. They started planning a bake sale that quickly transformed into the idea to hold a flea market. Props, costumes, and other items from the show were offered along with personal donations from the cast and crew, and $12,000 was raised. More than two decades later, the event draws upwards of 25,000 people in one day. Tables loaded with thousands of items line both sides of this city block. Major Broadway shows, theaters, unions, and off-Broadway theaters all participate.

This event is a theater lover's goldmine. You might find a baseball cap from *The Little Mermaid* for $2, a prop from *Avenue Q* for $50, a pair of sandals worn by Maria in *West Side Story* for $250, or a handmade Broadway Bear dressed like your favorite show character with a $1200 price tag. There are vintage *Playbills*, scripts, and show posters for sale, as well as memorabilia and props.

If you are an autograph hound, you can meet Broadway and TV stars all day long at the Celebrity Table. The schedule of who will be signing autographs at what time is available online in advance so that you can plan your visit. At one point in 2009 Chita Rivera and Bernadette Peters were signing autographs at the same time. Others included Harvey Fierstein, John Stamos, Tovah Feldshuh, *American Idol's* Constantine Maroulis and Diana DeGarmo, and many more.

The Grand Auction offers opportunities to experience things most people don't even dream about. In 2008, two lucky bidders won the chance to hang out with Daniel Radcliffe (Harry Potter), who starred in *Equus* on Broadway. Another bidder won the chance to appear on Broadway in the wedding scene in *Mamma Mia*. Someone else bought the opportunity to conduct the orchestra during the exit music of *The Phantom of the Opera*, another couple to spend the day on the set of *Ugly Betty*, and two others VIP tickets to see *Saturday Night Live* plus take a backstage tour with the director.

Crafts on Columbus

Columbus Avenue (77th St. / 81st St.)
Last weekend in April and first two weekends in May,
three weekends in October
10 am to 5:30 pm
1 to 79th Street, C to 81st Street-Museum of Natural History
www.craftsoncolumbus.com

The American Arts and Crafts Alliance presents two outdoor arts and crafts markets each year, one in spring and one in fall. The setting is lovely for a stroll among the more than one hundred tents erected along Columbus Avenue under the stately London plane trees next to the American Museum of Natural History, one block away from Central Park.

The first Crafts on Columbus market took place in 1979. Since then, the market has grown to include American artisans from the New York area and the rest of the country, including glassblowers, sculptors, jewelry designers, clothing designers, painters, and more.

The market takes place on property owned by the NYC Department of Parks & Recreation, so there are no food vendors. No need to fret. The neighborhood is chock-full of excellent restaurants. The GreenFlea market and the Columbus Avenue Greenmarket, both only a block away, are also places to find delicious and healthy snacks.

Treasures of the Vine (www.treasuresofthevine.com)
Treasures off the Vine upcycles wine and spirits bottles
and transforms them, with labels still intact, into cheese
platters. Vineyards across the country sell these glass platters that Treasures of the Vine makes from the vineyards'
own bottles.

C. Joseph Haberdasher for Men & Women
(www.catherinejoseph.com) Catherine Joseph's clothes
are expertly designed and stitched in wool and cashmere.
In addition to women's jackets and scarves in butter-soft
cashmere, tweed, and silk, Joseph designs "The Distin-
guished Shirt," a men's garment that serves double duty
as a warm woolen shirt and a stylish jacket. Record producer Tommy Mottola and software entrepreneur James
Wesolowski are among her clients.

Ekologic (www.ekologic.com) Ekologic's designer, Kathleen Tesnakis, uses textile waste from the garment industry to create handmade, one-of-a-kind clothes and accessories. She selects colorful cashmere knits to make dresses and shirts for women, as well as sweaters, hats, and mittens for men and children as well. Her accessories were selected for *Time's* "Green Gift List," and featured in *Organic Style* and on "Daily Candy."

Dudley Vaccianna Dudley Vaccianna creates paintings on hand-blown glass vases. Originally from Jamaica, Vaccianna paints detailed images of the faces and stories of his homeland. He works out of his studio in Brooklyn, where he partners with glassblowers to create the delicate glass canvasses.

Agneta P (www.nordicaffair.com) This hat and accessories designer knits wool-blend hats in jewel tones in intricate patterns. She also makes felt hats reminiscent of the twenties and thirties, but with a distinctly modern flair. Bergdorf Goodman has carried her lines.

Amazing Mobiles (www.amazing-mobiles.com) These handmade works of art turn simple bits of wire into dynamic vignettes with lifelike movements. Many of the mobiles depict people playing musical instruments. In one, a drum, a face, and two hands holding drumsticks all hang so that no matter which way the breeze blows, the hands play on the drum as the face looks on. The keyboard and banjo players are equally clever, as is the fellow blowing a kiss to the wind.

Ian Lander Jewelry (www.ianlander.com) Using metals, unusual stones, and macramé, this jewelry designer creates pieces that he describes as both urban and ethnic. The macramé necklaces and bracelets are made of finely knotted cord in rich earth tone colors combined with colorful semiprecious cabochons and beads. Lander's signature "Sun" pendant features round stones in a radiant solar setting.

London Terrace Street Fair

West 24th Street (Ninth Ave. / Tenth Ave.)
Annually in September 10 am to 6 pm
(check www.marketsofnewyork.com for dates)
1, C, E to 23rd Street

Usually, when New Yorkers hear the term "street fair," they think of the large, corporate-run events that take place along the streets and avenues of Manhattan. These street fairs all have the same food and the same vendors selling cheap mass-produced items, with rarely anything local or handmade to be found. Lots of people flock to these fairs, but many find them to be a significant nuisance. The London Terrace Street Fair is nothing like these.

London Terrace is an enormous apartment building that takes up an entire city block in the Chelsea neighborhood in Manhattan. The London Terrace Street Fair has taken place every September since 1992, with the single exception of 2001 when 24th Street was open only to emergency vehicles responding to the events of September 11th. Each year, residents and neighbors of the building clear out their closets and take all of the items they no longer want out onto the street to sell—and often to replace them with things they find at their neighbors' booths. This event is much like an old-fashioned swap meet or stoop sale—only with the equivalent of hundreds of stoops involved. (Note: In New York, the term "stoop sale" is akin to "garage sale" and "yard sale" in other parts of the country. Most residents do not have garages or yards, so they sell their belongings on the front stoop of their brownstones or apartment buildings.)

You can find incredibly good deals out on 24th Street. There are several antiques dealers there each year, as well as artisans selling handmade creations, but the vast majority of sellers are residents of the building. You will find furniture, toys, clothing, shoes, collectibles, electronics, antiques, kitchenware, jewelry, vintage buttons, and much more. I deeply regret not getting my hands on a pair of Frye boots before a young woman whisked them off for $10, but I did come home with a mint condition silk and angora cable knit sweater for $2. You might find a book you've been seeking for years, or a new favorite lamp. Next year I plan to search for a kimono.

Hardcore shoppers start arriving at 6 a.m. Most of the vendors are set up and eager to sell by 8:30, so if you are an early bird, you will not be disappointed. I like to get there at around 11:00 when things start to get busy. I've spent hours there, walking up and down the block a minimum of four times and finding something new with each pass. By late afternoon, around 4:30, the vendors are about ready to go home, and they do not want to bring their things back upstairs. At that time, the pickings may be slim, but bargains abound.

Washington Square Outdoor Art Exhibit

Washington Square, University Place (W. 3rd St. / E. 10th St.)

Memorial Day and Labor Day weekends, noon to 6 pm

R, W to 8th Street-New York University;

A, B, C, D, E, F, V to West 4th Street

www.washingtonsquareoutdoorartexhibit.org

The Washington Square Outdoor Art Exhibit had a humble yet auspicious beginning in 1931 during the Great Depression. In order to pay their rent, artists Jackson Pollock and Willem de Kooning took their paintings to sell in the Square. Citizens and the art world took note, more shows were organized, and the sales evolved into what eventually became the Outdoor Art Exhibit. It is now a biannual event, taking place over four weekends around Memorial Day in May and Labor Day in September.

Eighty years later, this event attracts more than two hundred artists and artisans to the square and surrounding streets. Thousands of visitors from around the world—and the neighborhood—include collectors, agents, gallery owners, restaurateurs, interior designers, and art lovers. The works exhibited are primarily paintings, sculpture, and photography. There is a separate area for crafts. Participants are invited by a jury; the jury also awards prizes in multiple categories.

Linda B. Cromer (www.lindabcromerwatercolors.com)
Linda Cromer is a Greenwich Village artist who paints vivid watercolor still lifes of fruit, flowers, and colorful striped and patterned textiles. It is difficult to walk by her table without being drawn in by her paintings of bright red amaryllises, lacy yellow irises, and delicate pink and burgundy cosmos blossoms.

Michael Chen Photography (www.mc-images.com)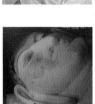
Michael Chen's portfolio includes images of people, places, and monuments from around the world: Cambodian monks praying at dawn in bright saffron-colored robes, a camel caravan crossing the Mongolian desert, the Chrysler Building glistening in a series of six photographs taken at different times of the day.

Richard Stalter (www.richardstalter.com) Richard Stalter
has participated in the Outdoor Art Exhibit since 1969. He paints landscapes, seascapes, still lifes, figures, and cityscapes. His paintings of county fairs first drew me into his exhibit space.

Ken Orton (www.kenortongallery.com) Ken Orton hails
from Birmingham, England, and lives in New York. He creates large photo-realistic paintings. In his series "Preserved Light" he has painted vintage glassware, capturing every glint of light and variation of color. "Lost Toys" is a group of paintings of abandoned mid-century cars and trucks.

Annual and Semi-Annual Markets
Brooklyn

Bust Magazine Craftaculars

www.bust.com (under events tab)
Spring Fling Craftacular and Holiday Craftacular
check website for details

B*ust* magazine ("For women with something to get off their chests") sponsored the first *Bust* Craftacular in 2003 to provide young female artisan/entrepreneurs with an event at which to sell their products and build their brands. Today, there are two Craftaculars per year, the Spring Fling in April and the Holiday Craftacular in December. A $2 admission fee includes a goodie bag, a chance to win raffle prizes, and a free copy of *Bust*.

The Spring Fling is held in Williamsburg at Warsaw, which is located at the Polish National Home. The large hall is filled with more than fifty exhibitors from across the country, now both men and women, selling handmade soaps, clothing, T-shirts, prints, metal wares, wooden objects, and cupcakes. There is a DJ spinning discs, and a beer tap running. The vibe is funky and artsy, just like Williamsburg itself.

The Holiday Craftacular is significantly larger. It is held in the big and bright Metropolitan Pavilion in Chelsea, one of New York City's premier event spaces. Thousands of people come to this event, which features vendors—and also thumping music, food, prizes, and more. It will take a while to wander down the aisles and examine all the handicrafts, so grab a cupcake, shake your booty, and get your holiday shopping done early.

The Renegade Craft Fair

McCarren Park, Greenpoint, Brooklyn
Saturday and Sunday in early June (check website for details)
L to Bedford Avenue, G to Nassau Avenue
www.renegadecraft.com

The Renegade Craft Fair has been an annual event in Brooklyn since 2006. Founder Sue Daly organized the first Renegade Craft Fair in Chicago in 2003. Since then, Renegades have been staged in Los Angeles, San Francisco, Chicago, and New York. Two holiday craft fairs are held in Chicago and San Francisco, and an online store (www.renegadehandmade.com) has recently been launched.

The Brooklyn Renegade is one of the largest, if not the largest, outdoor crafts market in town. The 2009 featured three hundred independent crafters from all parts of the country. Thousands of people flock to this event. In addition to the extensive array of handmade treasures, live music and food are provided. In 2009, the Treats Truck kept the crowds fed and happy all weekend long (www.treatstruck.com).

You'll find clothing for men, women, and especially for children, leather bags and fabric totes, ceramics and glass, stationery and jewelry galore. Some of my favorite New York designers participate in the Renegade Craft Fair: Alison Tauber, Angelrox, Digby & Iona, Fine and Raw Chocolate, Gnome Enterprises, KnitKnit, k*, Rocks & Salt, Seibei, and the New New. Hundreds of other artisans offer unique and wonderful crafts as well, including: Bunny Butt Apothecary, Tugboat Print Shop, Squidfire, Pinkypunk, Enfant Terrible, and Argyle Whale.

Brooklyn Lyceum Craft Markets

227 Fourth Avenue (President St. / Union St.)

Park Slope, Brooklyn

Spring and holidays (check website for details)

R to Union Street

www.bkcraftcentral.com and www.brooklynlyceum.com

A former public bath, the Brooklyn Lyceum was abandoned for many years until it reopened in 2002 as an arts venue featuring dance, theater, arts, movies, music, festivals, and more. The space—gritty and functional—supports many community, family, food, and arts-oriented events.

The Lyceum holds craft markets each year in spring and winter. In March 2009, a craft market, "'Specially for Kids," was held, offering toys, clothes, and other items exclusively for children. You'll always find local purveyors selling their "crafty" cupcakes, chocolates, and sandwiches. The Lyceum's café has delicious baked goods and serves Intelligentsia tea and coffee.

The market is arranged in such as a way as to allow for comfortable strolling, browsing, and shopping; the aisles are wide. The majority of tables are in the large event space downstairs, but don't overlook the additional alcoves upstairs; large handmade signs will help you find your way.

The markets attract some of the finest craft workers in the city and the east coast. The creations I have seen there are beautifully made and often quite witty.

Lovely Day Designs sells hand-poured soy candles in vintage teacups, pressed-glass votives, and porcelain gravy boats, as well other decorative items. One of the more unusual things I came across was the living jewelry from McFlashpants, tiny plants rooted in miniscule vials hanging as pendants on a necklace. Everything Tiny creates laser cut accessories using bright colors and fun images such as dinosaurs, Legos, deer, and dachshunds. Pickleboots has clever things for kids, including an art apron filled with crayons.

Girls Can Tell creates graphic images printed on pages torn from books. The soaps from Nordea all smell divine; the felted scrubber soaps in bright colors would be great stocking stuffers. Framed prints from Raw Toast Design are colorful, skillfully drawn, and darkly funny, like the "poor calamari" being eaten by seagulls. For really great T-shirts, I couldn't resist the bright pink giant squid from Squidfire. Miss Wit lives up to her name with T-shirts with nostalgic '80s themes.

The perfect
antidote to
the 9 to 5.

Holiday Markets

Holiday Markets
Manhattan

Columbus Circle Holiday Market

West 59th Street and Central Park West

Monday to Saturday, 10 am to 8 pm; Sunday 10 am to 7 pm

Holiday season through Christmas Eve

1, A, B, C, D to 59th Street-Columbus Circle

www.nycgovparks.org/parks/centralpark

Central Park is lovely year round, and it is particularly splendid after a wintry snowfall. The horse-drawn carriages clip-clop through the park, wending their way over snow-covered bridges and streets, evoking a Currier & Ives print. The Holiday Market's festive tents and garlands are a sight to behold, especially toward evening when the lights sparkle.

Although this market is organized by the same group that runs the Union Square Holiday Market, the Columbus Circle Holiday Market is distinct and special. It is a destination in and of itself, and many people plan trips especially to shop here. Holiday visitors from the nearby hotels flock to the market to shop for special gifts from New York City. Note that the market generally opens the week after Thanksgiving because it is located on the route of the Macy's Thanksgiving Day Parade and cannot be constructed until after the event.

As with Union Square, the merchandise at the Columbus Circle Holiday Market is primarily local, with handicrafts from around the world as well. With over one hundred vendor booths to peruse, you will definitely not go home empty-handed.

You can choose from many different kinds of bath and body products to keep your skin glowing during the dry winter season. There are always perfumed candles and plenty of decorative items to make your home cozy and beautiful. For your favorite cooks, you can find olive oils and wines, as well as handmade cutting boards. There are many accessories to choose from, including handbags, leather belts, hats, gloves, and scarves of all sizes, shapes, and colors. Jewelry is always a major component of any market, and this one is no different. I have found long, beaded lariat necklaces, crystal earrings, and Scrabble tile cuff links. For pets, bright collar-and-leash sets, crazy toys filled with catnip, and cozy beds abound.

When your bags are full, you can buy a large cup of cocoa at the kiosk next to the market, pull down your ear flaps, and go for an invigorating stroll down the Poets' Walk to see if the Boat Pond is frozen. Finish up your perfect wintry day in Central Park with a skate at Wollman Rink, as New Yorkers have done since 1949.

Grand Central Terminal Holiday Fair

Vanderbilt Hall, Grand Central Terminal,

42nd Street & Lexington Avenue

Monday to Saturday, 10 am to 8 pm; Sunday 11 am to 7 pm

From Monday before Thanksgiving through December 24th

4, 5, 6, 7, S to Grand Central-42nd Street

www.grandcentralterminal.com

Grand Central Terminal's Holiday Fair opens the week of Thanksgiving in November, thus marking the start of the New York holiday season. Held in glorious Vanderbilt Hall, this market is unparalleled in the quality of its goods and the comfort of indoor shopping. This annual artisan and design market first started in 1998.

Vanderbilt Hall—with its iconic oval chandeliers and architecture—alone is worth the visit. No longer a waiting room for travelers, today the space is used for events such as corporate parties, art exhibits, car shows, travel expos, and an annual professional squash tournament. A public memorial service for Jackie Kennedy Onassis, who campaigned to save Grand Central Station from demolition, was held in Vanderbilt Hall in 1994.

The Holiday Fair is one market not to miss. The booths are cleverly designed to give shoppers the feeling that they are walking down a cozy street and into exclusive little boutiques. Each year, a marvelous mix of more than seventy vendors is carefully selected. You can find all sorts of jewelry designs, ranging from handmade ruby earrings to chunky silver rings made from the keys off an old typewriter. There are clothes,

costumes, and toys for children. Many vendors sell hats, scarves and gloves, as well as handbags and totebags. Housewares and decorative items are popular as well, as are holiday decorations.

It is easy to plan an entire afternoon of fun around the Holiday Fair. After you are finished shopping, you can wander into the grand concourse to watch the holiday light shows projected onto the Sky Ceiling. The New York Transit Museum sets up their annual Holiday Show, where model trains zip around the tracks set in a miniature New York City. There are more than thirty restaurants and specialty food stores throughout Grand Central to choose among.

The Union Square Holiday Market

Southwest corner of Union Square
(Near E. 14th St. and Union Sq. West.)
Monday to Friday, 11 am to 8 pm; Saturday 10 am to 8 pm;
Sunday 11 am to 7 pm
4, 5, 6, L, N, Q, R, W to 14th Street-Union Square
www.nycgovparks.org/parks/unionsquarepark

You can feel the chill in the air, and the red-and-white-striped tents are going up on Union Square at 14th Street. The holidays are here! The Union Square Holiday Market is a must-do destination for holiday shoppers. The festive atmosphere at the market, located at the southwestern end of the square, is hard to resist. You may feel as if you're wandering through a small village as you meander through the boutique tents that curve around the subway station pavilion.

First established in 1994, this market offers an enormous amount of variety. With more than one hundred vendors, the place is buzzing all day and well after dark.

The vendors are a carefully selected mix of local artisans and "global-local" merchandise (handcrafted goods from around the world). The merchandise is quite varied. The options for children of all ages are practically limitless: sweet tiny onesies for babies and small outfits in many different styles for toddlers. There are oodles of clever, educational, creative, and fun toys that will make children—and their parents—very happy. You'll find plenty of clothing, from skirts and dresses for women to jackets for men, and plenty of funny T-shirts.

You'll find clever hats: a sock monkey hat with a wool Mohawk, a fuzzy hat with kitty ears, and a large Mad Hatter hat. There are many more "serious" hats, as well, along with gloves and scarves in wool, felt, fleece, and silk.

There are food and drink vendors inside the market, but if you need to warm up and rest your feet, there are ample choices around Union Square for a full meal or delicious snack. You can ask anyone in Union Square, and each person will have a great suggestion. I must take this opportunity to make a suggestion of my own: The Donut Pub (14th Street at 7th Avenue), a beloved neighborhood spot where the donuts are made right in the back, and are always mouthwateringly fresh.

The Holiday Shops at Bryant Park

Between 40th and 42nd Streets and Fifth and Sixth Avenues,
behind the New York Public Library
Monday to Friday, 11 am to 8 pm; Saturday 10 am to 9 pm;
Sunday 10 am to 6 pm
Open approximately November 1 through January 1
B, D, F, V to 42nd Street-Bryant Park; 7 to 5th Avenue-Bryant Park
www.theholidayshopsatbryantpark.com

Bryant Park is stunningly beautiful on a regular day, but it goes all out for the holidays. Inspired by the traditional holiday markets in Vienna and Strasbourg, this market has been carefully designed to create a comfortable and festive atmosphere for shopping outdoors. You will notice the impressive glass booths, reminiscent of the Crystal Palace, which housed New York's first World's Fair in 1853–54 where Bryant Park now stands. This market has a perfect mix of shopping, entertainment, and food.

The 125 vendors are all selected by the market organizers with an emphasis on local and handmade artisanal merchandise. Some of the most compelling items I have seen at this market include: breathtakingly beautiful—and sharp—chef's knives from New West Knifeworks; quirky candy wrapper purses from Nahui Ollin; adorable handmade teddy bears from Tedde; and hand-hammered, hand-tooled, hand-designed belts from Jon Wye.

This is also a great market for eco-friendly gifts. You can try on clothes made from organic, recycled, and upcycled materials from Mama

Shaman. Metal Park makes sculptures from recycled metal. Probably the most unusual products at this market are high-quality recycled paper products (cards, stationery, and more) by Mr. Elliepoo. Their paper is made from 100% recycled elephant, rhino, and reindeer poo. Really. And the list goes on.

There are abundant food options within the market. Of course there is steaming hot cocoa. You can bite into a candied apple, or a piece of Max Brenner chocolate. If you want a savory snack, there are soups and sandwiches. I highly recommend the mozzarepa, a traditional South American arepa, or cornbread patty, filled with hot, melted mozzarella cheese.

For more formal dining, step inside Celsius: A Canadian Lounge, a full restaurant and bar constructed just for this market. You can sit indoors or outside on the terrace, complete with heat lamps. Lunch, dinner, and snacks are served. Finally, to wrap up your visit to Bryant Park, you can rent skates and go for a glide on The Pond, the seasonal skating rink in the center of the market.

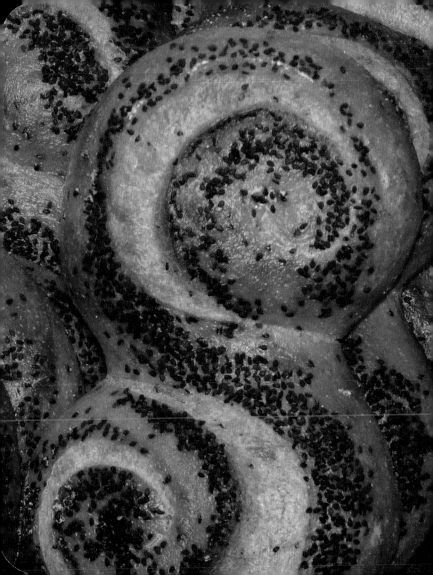

Food Markets

Food Markets
Manhattan

Chelsea Market

75 Ninth Avenue (W. 15th St. / W. 16th St.)
Monday to Saturday, 7 am to 10 pm; Sunday 8 am to 8 pm
1, 2, 3, A, C, E to 14th Street, L to Eighth Avenue
www.chelseamarket.com

The first Oreo was made in the former Nabisco factory that now houses Chelsea Market. Vanilla Wafers, Fig Newtons, Barnum's Animal Crackers, and Premium Saltines were also made in the same building, where the current occupants are a fitting tribute to the culinary tradition. More than twenty-nine retail shops and restaurants in the complex provide a rich mix of every kind of food item, whether you are shopping for groceries or creating a picnic to take to the nearby High Line Elevated Park.

Four bakeries sell fresh bread, pastries, and other baked goods. Assemble a "surf and turf" dinner with seafood from The Lobster Place and cuts of local grass-fed beef from Dickson's Farmstand Meats. Desserts are in abundance, from elaborately decorated cookies to Italian gelato.

You can also have memorable meals at the market. Breakfast at Sarabeth's Kitchen can be a fresh blueberry muffin with a dollop of the signature preserves. At lunch, belly up to the milk bar at Ronnybrook Dairy for a chicken salad sandwich with apples and celery, followed by a scoop (or two) of rich chocolate ice cream. If you need an afternoon snack, pick up a juicy Guss's pickle at Friedman's Lunch, a cup of tea at T Salon, or chocolates from Jacques Torres. Dinner options range from beyond-trendy Buddakan, to the Iron Chef's Morimoto, and 202, the New York outpost of designer/restauranteuse Nicole Farhi. For a more intimate setting, try the Green Table inside the market itself for "farm to table cuisine."

Chelsea Market is also the headquarters of the Food Network, and its food stores supply ingredients to world-class chefs, many of whom film their shows in the studios upstairs.

Chelsea Market Baskets (www.chelseamarketbaskets. com) Chelsea Market Baskets is the shop to visit for jellies, jams, and chutneys, as well as crackers, chips, and cheeses. Don't miss the glass cases filled with Leonidas chocolates, especially around Easter, Halloween, Valentine's Day, or any holiday—you'll be sure to find a mouth-watering selection of sweet treats. Everything you choose can be beautifully packed in a gift basket, or the staff can make suggestions along a theme: New Home, Thank You, Sympathy, Wedding, and more. There are eight New York City-themed basket choices, or create your own.

Bowery Kitchen Supply (www.bowerykitchens.com) The shelves and bins at Bowery Kitchen Supply overflow with every kind of kitchen gadget and doodad to help you cook to perfection. You can find heavy-duty skillets and utensils, commercial muffin pans, knives of every shape, and style, mixers and blenders, strainers, kitchen crocs and chef apparel, cutlery, ceramic crème brûlée pots, and chopsticks—the list goes on and on. There's also a great deli on-site, Bowery Eats. This shop is known as "where the chefs shop," and it is true—on one day, within twenty minutes, I saw no fewer than five chefs from nearby restaurants or The Food Network come into the store for particular items.

Amy's Bread (www.amysbread.com) If you time it just right, you can pick up a warm, crispy baguette or a buttery brioche loaf as it comes right out of the oven at Amy's. The cherry scones are moist and crumbly, and there is little way to resist the golden brown sticky buns. At the small café, you can try Amy's delicious prepared sandwiches and salads, followed by a chewy chocolate chip cookie and a cup of coffee. Each year, my birthday cake comes from Amy's.

Buon Italia (www.buonitalia.com) This family-owned business carries hundreds of Italian delicacies, many of which find their way to the tables of the city's Italian restaurants. You will find traditional pastas, tomato sauces, olive oils, and vinegars. In the cold case, look for paper-thin slices of imported mortadella and prosciutto cotto, as well as cheeses that arrive weekly from Italy. Most of Buon Italia's pastas come from Setaro, a small artisanal factory in Naples, where the pasta is dried naturally in rooms made from volcanic stone rather than in industrial driers.

Hale and Hearty Soups (www.haleandhearty.com) Hale and Hearty Soups specializes in the ultimate comfort food, hot soup, served with a side of bread or oyster crackers. All are rich and, well, hearty; standouts include mac and cheese and beef, lobster bisque, old-fashioned chicken and dumpling, and Senegalese beef and peanut—my all-time favorite. The salad bar is loaded with different fixings, with dressings made from scratch. New soups are introduced each week and the menu changes daily; check the website. Hale and Hearty accepts requests for specific soups to be put on the menu. Tomato cheddar is the most requested.

Manhattan Fruit Exchange This greengrocer carries a tremendous variety of foods to accommodate the diverse needs of more than two hundred restaurant clients, available to the public at prices just above wholesale. MFE stocks seasonal fruits and vegetables (it's not unusual to find thirty varieties of mushrooms) as well as herbs, cheeses, sausages, spices, legumes, nuts, dried fruits, and more. You'll find a large organic produce section, a salad bar, and freshly squeezed juices.

Jacques Torres Chocolates
(www.jacquestorreschocolate.com) "Eat Dessert First" is the motto of master chocolatier Jacques Torres, who makes both the classics (champagne truffles, caramel nut noir, and dark chocolate ganache) as well as chocolates with a decidedly modern approach (pineapple pastis, chai tea, and red wine Grand Cru). In addition to running his chocolate shops, Torres serves as Dean of Pastry Arts at the French Culinary Institute.

Chelsea Wine Vault (www.chelseawinevault.com) This warm and charming wine shop started as a wine storage facility for New York's wine collectors. Private collections are still stored here in underground vaults, with a staff to tend to them. The same staff can help you find the perfect bottle—or two. The shop likes to stock wine from small producers and growers around the world, and can accommodate any budget. On one end of the spectrum is the selection of ninety-nine $9.99 bottles displayed throughout the store. On the other end is a collection of vintage champagnes, including festive and gigantic Salmanazars and Nebuchadnezzars. Chelsea Wine Vault is the go-to wine retailer for *Food & Wine* and for The Food Network.

Samurai Sharpening (www.samuraisharpening.com) Perhaps only the glint of a steel blade will prevent you from walking right by the small table that has become a popular place to have knives sharpened. Knife expert Margery Cohen has been sharpening knives every Wednesday and Saturday outside the Bowery Kitchen Supply store since 1997. People come from far and wide to drop off their Wustoffs and Henckels, often sheathed in nothing but a kitchen towel. By the time they are done shopping and having a cup of gelato, their knives are razor sharp.

Essex Street Market

120 Essex Street (at Delancey St.)
Monday to Saturday, 8 am to 7 pm
J, M, Z to Essex Street; F to Delancey Street
www.essexstreetmarket.com

In the 1940s, Mayor Fiorello La Guardia found that vendors selling their wares from pushcarts were hindering traffic flow, so he built several indoor markets where vendors could set up their shops and sell their wares off the streets and out of the weather. The Essex Street Market in the heart of the Lower East Side of Manhattan was one of those markets.

In the first half of the twentieth century, the residents of the Lower East Side were primarily Jewish and Italian immigrants. The Essex Street Market reflected those demographics in the products sold there. In the latter part of the century, the new immigrants were Puerto Rican and Dominican. It remains a largely Hispanic neighborhood, but there are now people from all over the world, including young professionals, students, and families.

Long a mainstay in the community, the market encountered years of hardship in the seventies and eighties when new, modern supermarkets moved into the neighborhood. Luckily, it survived until 1995, when the New York City Economic Development Commission invested in a major renovation of the facilities.

Today, the market is better than ever, with a mixture of Old World food purveyors and new entrepreneurs. Twenty-four vendors sell an array of meat, fish, gourmet foods, produce, and groceries; two restaurants, an art gallery, a barber, a clothing shop, and an electronics store fill the rest of the space. As you wander through the aisles, the vendors will answer your questions and often give you a taste of something yummy. And maybe, if you're lucky, Jeffrey Ruhalter, a fourth-generation butcher, might toss you an apron and invite you to see what life is like behind the counter at the Essex Street Market.

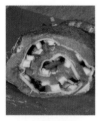

Jeffrey's Meats (www.jeffreysonessex.com) Jeffrey Ruhalter's great-grandfather was a butcher on the Lower East Side in the 1920s. Jeffrey has followed in his footsteps—and then some. In addition to running the retail shop, he sells wholesale to some of New York's finest restaurants and to many celebrity chefs, hosts dinners for the community, and presents exhibitions by local artists in his shop.

Three Brothers Clothing If you are looking for a particular item, be it a party dress or a blazer, stop by and see what Three Brothers has on the racks and shelves that are miraculously squeezed into this small space. You'll also find jewelry, shoes, cosmetics, perfumes, and more.

Roni-Sue's Chocolates (www.roni-sue.com) Chocolatier Rhonda Kave makes her sweet delicacies by hand right in the market. Try her delightful seasonal rose-flavored truffle, or her butter crunch. She also sells collections of flavored bonbons, including "Cocktails" and "Chile Lovers." She is probably most famous for her bacon confections, such as chocolate-covered bacon strips, bacon butter crunch, and BaCorn, caramel popcorn with bacon and chile piñon nuts. The entire bacon line was recently picked up by Dean & Deluca. Rhonda's bacon comes from Jeffrey across the aisle.

Essex Farm Groceries You may be surprised to find exactly what you are looking for at this grocery store. Although small, it is well stocked, well organized, and has hundreds of products for cooking all different kinds of foods. There are rows of exotic spices and teas, and shelves of standard groceries, such as cereal, peanut butter, and pasta. There are typical fruits and vegetables displayed right alongside cactus leaves, yucca, and plantains. Whether you need some peanut butter and jelly or a jar of huitlacoche (Mexican corn mushrooms), you'll probably find it here.

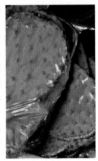

Formaggio Essex (www.formaggiokitchen.com) Based in Cambridge, Mass., Formaggio Kitchen describes itself as "a gourmand's paradise doubling as a neighborhood grocer." The shop in the Essex Street Market is about the size of a suburban walk-in closet, but it is chock-full of Old World Italian specialties—a selection of artisanal cheeses, numerous varieties of olives and antipasti, and pastas of all shapes and colors. Refill your olive oil and vinegar bottles from two large urns on the shelf.

Saxelby Cheesemongers (www.saxelbycheese.com) Anne Saxelby is a purveyor of "fine American farmstead cheese." In her tiny shop piled high with cheeses, look for the ashed goat cheese from Pipe Dreams Farm in Pennsylvania (one of my all-time favorites; if you see it, buy it—it sells out quickly). This cheesemonger can recommend a perfect cheese for any occasion, from nutty Vermont Shepherd and Pleasant Ridge Reserve, made from raw cow's milk, to "fudgy" Bayley Hazen Blue. "What's small and cardboard and smells like a sock?" A luscious mail order gift box of cheese from Saxelby Cheesemongers.

La Tiendita by the Lower Eastside Girls Club (www. girlsclub.org/store) La Tiendita is owned and run by the Lower Eastside Girls Club, a nonprofit organization dedicated to helping girls and young women develop confidence and leadership skills. Baking skills are taught at the Sweet Things Bake Shop and the baked goods are sold at La Tiendita ("the little shop") here at the Essex Street Market. You can buy cupcakes, brownies, cookies, Girl-Power bars, granola, pies, and more.

PER LB $20.99 WEST PARIST, VT
PER PIECE
DIAT, asparagus, not
Not at all what kind o
from looking at it bu
to catch - full bo
Made from

A little tart of a che
which is just how we
made from Holstein milk
bound in cloth, Landaff
- pucker and twang
me of the finest
from the British
als at JASPER

GRAYSON
Meadow Creek Dairy
$18.99 Galax, VA
PER LB
PER PIECE GOAT☐ SHEEP☐ COW☑
Rick and Helen Feete present
Grayson! The Feetes are
traditionalists when it comes
to milking their herd and
make cheese only when their
cows are out on grass...

Maple Smoked Gouda
TAYLOR FARM
$18.99 Londonderry, VT
PER LB
PER PIECE GOAT☐ SHEEP☐ COW☑
As close as you can get to
eating bacon without actually
eating bacon! Mild, succulent
and creamy, with a sweet
smoky flavor that'll knock
your socks off. Made from
good grass-fed Vermont
milk, ...

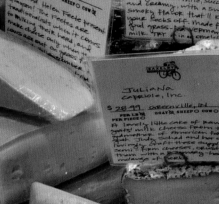

JuliaNa
Capriole, Inc.
$28.99 Greenville, IN
PER LB
PER PIECE GOAT☑ SHEEP☐ COW☐
A lovely little cake of raw
goat's milk cheese from the
Judy Schad and her crew
semi firm dressed, rubbed ...

HooLiGan
Cato Corner Farm
$25.99 Colchester, C
PER LB
PER PIECE GOAT☐ SHEEP☐ COW☑
A Real drug of a stinky
bomage - some have the
addicted to its wild an
odoriferous ways. This ra
cheese is aged for 60 day
the legal limit for raw c
cheese. Alsatian Munster-...

BROVETTO DAIRY
Harpersfield w/ommegang
$17.99 Jefferson, NY
PER LB
PER PIECE GOAT☐ SHEEP☐ COW☑
we like cheese. we like beer.
we like it even better when
they're melded together!
when this chees ...

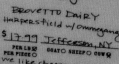

SNOW
field Farm
han, NY
SHEEP☐ COW☐
dle-licious ...

Willow
Ploughgate
$18.99
PER LB
PER PIECE
meet Willow
little stinker
of Vermont. T
is made fro
herd of Ho

Grand Central Market

Grand Central Terminal, 105 East 42nd Street at Lexington Avenue
Monday to Friday, 7 am to 9 pm; Saturday 10 am to 7 pm,
Sunday 11 am to 6 pm
4, 5, 6, 7, S to Grand Central-42nd Street
www.grandcentralterminal.com

Grand Central Terminal is one of New York's grandest landmark buildings. Inaugurated in 1913, Grand Central now has millions of commuters and visitors every year. When a New Yorker says, "Meet me at the clock," fellow Gothamites know that the rendezvous point is the information kiosk under the famous brass clock in the center of the Grand Concourse, the traditional meeting place for lunch dates and visiting relatives.

It is almost impossible to believe that Grand Central Terminal came perilously close to the wrecking ball—until Jacqueline Kennedy Onassis and other city leaders took action to save this glorious building. It was designated a National Historic Landmark by the National Register of Historic Places in 1978.

In 1999, the doors opened on Grand Central Market, a food shopper's dream and the perfect place to pick up something tasty, fresh, and healthy for breakfast, lunch, and dinner. Thirteen shops overflow with everything you need to pack a picnic for a concert in Central Park or to whip up a gourmet dinner when you get home. There are two fruit and vegetable stands, a classic Italian butcher, two bakeries, two fishmongers, a branch of a celebrated New York City-based chocolate shop, a coffee shop, a spice shop, and more. Many of these shops are New York institutions selling locally produced delicacies.

You can stroll from one end of the market to the other and back again, thinking up new recipes, getting cooking tips, and filling up your shopping bag with a crunchy baguette, a jar of caviar, a dry-aged T-bone, a robust Jersey tomato, and a box of chocolate truffles for dessert.

Murray's Cheese and Real Salami (www.murrayscheese.com) These are two fully stocked outposts of Murray's Cheese, a New York institution on Bleecker Street in the Village. The cheese shop sells Murray's selections from across the U.S. and Europe. Real Salami sells artisanal sausages, pâtés, smoked meats, and more. Signs provide short and pithy descriptions of the origins and flavors of each delectable product, and tasting is encouraged.

Greenwich Produce Pick up some apples and a dozen daisies for your home, desk, or hotel room. Fresh produce marts at both ends of the market sell prepackaged selections that make it easy to grab a healthy snack on the go. You'll find a flower stand at the Lexington Street entrance.

Pescatore Seafood Company (www.allfreshseafood. com) Glen Licht and Jerry Bocchino offer a wide variety of fresh seafood, both prepared and ready to cook. They also have great daily specials, such as two-for-one salmon cakes, and on occasion, buy-one-ounce-of-caviar-get-one-free. They recently launched their own line of flavored panko that has become a must-have item in my kitchen.

Zaro's Bread Basket (www.zaro.com) Another New York Institution, Zaro's has been providing breads, sandwiches, and sweets to New York City for more than seventy-five years. All baking is done at a large facility in the Bronx and delivered to the stores twice a day. Zaro's babka, bagels, and rugelach are part of the city's culinary culture. At the Grand Central Market location, you can find homemade Old World-style breads, black and white cookies, and much more.

Penzey's Spices (www.penzeys.com) Penzey's warm wooden shelves are laden with the shop's signature pale yellow-labeled bottles of familiar and exotic spices. Penzey's spices are all chemical-free and sourced directly from producers around the world. Knowledgeable salespeople are happy to help you find the perfect ingredients for your favorite recipes. I like their gift box collections, including "Spicy Wedding" and "American Kitchen," which come in boxes sprinkled with loose bay leaves and nutmegs.

Koglin Royal German Hams (www.koglinroyalhams. com) For German expatriates in New York and lovers of German food alike, Koglin's is a lifeline to Germany's delicacies. Mr. Koglin, dubbed the King of Hams by his customers, sells thirty different kinds of hams and twenty-five types of salami—the largest selection in the U.S. You can also find salted herring, homemade sauerkraut, and German potato salad, among the hundreds of items. Diehards: Koglin's ham lard is said to be delicious on bread.

Wild Edibles (www.wildedibles.com) Wild Edibles sells fresh seafood, including fish (some of it organic), shellfish, salts, and seasonings. The most current information from the Blue Ocean Institute about the origins and environmental status of each item for sale is posted in the store, which is committed to sourcing fish that has been responsibly harvested.

Ceriello Fine Foods (www.ceriellofinefoods.com) Ceriello is a classic Italian butcher shop and purveyor of Italian foods. The butchers will prepare your dry-aged sirloin while you peruse the sausages, tangy sauces, and handmade antipasti. If you don't feel like cooking, choose a rotisserie chicken or barbecued pork for an easy dinner.

Li-Lac Chocolates (www.li-lacchocolates.com) First established in 1923, Li-Lac Chocolates has been tickling New York's sweet tooth for almost a century with a luscious variety of chocolates made in its Brooklyn factory. Li-Lac's glass cases are filled with simple bars, bonbons, cream rolls, chocolate covered fruits, and my favorite, chocolate-covered Oreo cookies, as well as fun molded chocolates— you can bite the art deco spire off the top of a milk chocolate Empire State Building.

Corrado Bakery (www.corradobread.com) Beautiful pastries and fresh breads fill the cases and shelves at Corrado Bakery, which is known for organic breads and petits fours, among the dozens of mouthwatering baked goods.

Oren's Daily Roast (www.orensdailyroast.com) Smooth and fragrant, Oren's coffees are grown around the world and roasted daily right across the river in Jersey City, New Jersey. This shop sells beans only; if you want a cup of Oren's coffee, look for the eight shops around town. Owner Oren Bloostein is committed to buying directly from local growers to ensure a fair exchange. Oren's New York City Blend was developed after 9/11, and served for weeks without charge to rescue workers and volunteers at Ground Zero during the recovery efforts.

Dishes At Home (www.dishestogo.com) If you are not a cook but still love delicious food, a daily stop at Dishes is in order. Platters of freshly cooked mains and savory sides appear at lunchtime. The staff is happy to let you sample a few dishes before you decide.

New Amsterdam Market

Fulton Fish Market, South Street (Beekman St. / Peck Slip)
(check website for dates and times)
2, 3, 4, 5, J, M, Z to Fulton Street; A, C to Broadway-Nassau Street
www.newamsterdammarket.org

New Amsterdam showcases regional food purveyors. Its organizers aim to revive the tradition of markets where one can find fresh, local, and diverse food all in one public space. While the market does not yet have a fixed location or schedule, the objective is to move it permanently into the old Fulton Fish Market facility in the South Street Seaport. For now, check the website or sign up for e-mail notifications to see exactly where and when the market will be held.

More than ninety vendors from upstate New York, New Jersey, Connecticut, New Hampshire, Vermont, and other nearby locations usually participate. Among the stalls you may find artisanal breads, handmade fruit preserves, juices, and honey. There will also be butchers with specialties including American bison products, grass-fed and organic livestock, and jerkies. Regional dairies supply yogurt and milk, and the variety of delicious small-batch cheeses is vast. There are pastry makers, chocolatiers, confectioners, and purveyors of seasonal fruit and vegetables. There are also sandwiches, soups, and other prepared foods. There is a wonderful energy at this market, and the commitment to quality is evident in every display of amazing edibles.

Basis—Good Food for All (www.basisfoods.com)
Basis sells milk and yogurt, local honey, eggs, and produce. Basis partners with producers and local communities to sell good food—traditional, localized, and 100% traceable—at affordable prices. Basis works with farmers to find a market for all the food they produce, and provides delivery, storage and marketing services for them to sell directly to wholesale customers, including restaurants and retailers. Basis is opening a new chain of small-format retail stores, starting in New York City.

Maple Hill Creamery (www.maplehillcreamery.com)
Maple Hill Creamery produces small-batch milk, yogurt, and cheese products from grass-fed animals. Yogurts are sweet and creamy with that classic yogurt bite that is often missing in national-brand yogurt.

Fleisher's Grass-fed & Organic Meats
(www.fleishers.com) Owners Joshua Applestone, a fifth generation butcher, and Jessica Applestone come to the market with coolers loaded with gorgeous cuts of organic and grass-fed beef, pork, lamb, and poultry, as well as cheese. Fleisher's has been on Saveur's Top 100 list and sells meats to some of the region's best restaurants, including Blue Hill.

Fine & Raw Chocolate (www.fineandraw.com) Chocolatier and founder Daniel Sklaar has a background as a raw chef. The chocolates he makes include no sugar, dairy, or additives, and are prepared at the lowest possible heat in order to maintain flavor and antioxidants. Sklaar uses blue agave nectar for sweetening, and all ingredients are organic or wild-crafted.

Balthazar Bakery (www.balthazarbakery.com) This bakery not only supplies the brasserie Balthazar, but brings piles of fresh bread to the New Amsterdam Market. Balthazar's goods are made using traditional French techniques, and they can be found in the premier restaurants, hotels, and gourmet shops in the city. The bakery made Halve Maen Pies especially for the New Amsterdam Market in homage to the ship Henry Hudson sailed to the New World, the Half Moon.

Bellwether Hard Cider (www.cidery.com) Bellwether produces handcrafted hard cider using traditional techniques from France and England and apples from the cidery's own pesticide-free orchards as well as different varieties from other local orchards in New York State's Finger Lakes region. Bellwether currently offers ten flavors of hard cider, including the semi-dry Spyglass, the dry Lord Scudamore, and the semi-sweet Black Magic. The cider maker has been part of the Cayuga Lake Wine Trail for several years.

The Redhead (www.theredheadnyc.com) Partners Meg Grace, Gregg Nelson, and Rob Larcom's specialty, Bacon Peanut Brittle, has caused a lot of buzz at the market. If you want to try the bacon peanut brittle before the next market, it's on the menu of their restaurant (The Redhead at 349 East 13th St.), and available online.

Food Markets
Brooklyn

Moore Street Market / La Marqueta

110 Moore Street (between Humboldt St. and Graham Ave.),
East Williamsburg
Monday to Thursday 8 am to 6 pm, Friday & Saturday 8 am to 7 pm,
Sunday 10 am to 5 pm
J to Flushing Avenue, M weekdays, L to Montrose Avenue
www.bedc.org/subsidiaries/moore-street-market

The Moore Street Market, also known as La Marqueta de Williamsburg, is undergoing a renaissance. Another of the markets created by Mayor La Guardia in 1941, the Moore Street Market almost closed in 2007, but lingered on. In 2009, due to public outcry and support, it received a reprieve and a beauty makeover, and it is open for business seven days a week.

The market is located in the heart of East Williamsburg, which, in all honesty, is not the most beautiful part of Brooklyn. However, if you are a chowhound or a cook looking for unusual ingredients, the market is definitely worth a visit. Here you can find fresh produce, including exotic root vegetables, and dozens of herbs and spices for cooking and medicinal purposes. Have a delicious lunch and round out your experience by getting your hair cut by an old-fashioned barber. There are currently thirteen vendors with room to add several more.

The neighborhood is primarily Hispanic, with residents from throughout Latin America and the Caribbean. As you sit and have lunch under a cheery umbrella in the public dining area, you will see old men chatting about politics, young families with children running around the market's nooks and crannies, and serious food shoppers. La Marqueta serves the community by providing spaces to meet friends, hosting music events, providing health screening and nutrition education, and more. It definitely helps if you speak Spanish, but it is not necessary.

Note: There is another market known as La Marqueta in Spanish Harlem, which once featured more than 450 vendors. As of this writing there are only six; it is not included in this guide.

La Marketa Music Center If you love to dance, you won't be able to help yourself at this shop, where you can find the latest sounds of merengue, salsa, balada, and bachata amidst the thousands of new CDs on the shelves and along the walls. The proprietor can help you find the classics, too.

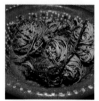

Las Gemelas Herbs and Spices The shelves of this shop are stacked with plastic containers holding hundreds of herbs. The owner is familiar with medicinal herbs, so she can recommend individual herbs or herbal blends for whatever ails you. I like to pick up small bags of cooking herbs and tisanes, such as oregano, cumin, mint, and chamomile.

Abby's Food Market Abby's carries local and imported fruits and vegetables, from potatoes and onions to *savila* (aloe) and plantains. You can also find freshly made green sofrito, as well as Puerto Rican sweets and coconut milk.

Botanica La Esperanza Proprietor Maria Esperanza says she can advise you in affairs of the heart, how to attract good luck, or remove an evil spell. Her shop has rows and rows of fascinating candles, perfumes, and statuettes of saints.

Maryzuh Flowers & Gifts Hosting a Sweet Sixteen or a Quinceañera Party? Maryzuh has a huge selection of extremely colorful cake toppers, silk florals, and ribbons.

Ocasio Craftsman You don't have to go to Puerto Rico to buy fun souvenirs. Ocasio Craftsman sells handmade wooden plaques with typical symbols of Puerto Rico, as well as key rings, flags, and other ways to display your love of the island.

Feeling hungry at the Market?

American Coffee Shop A mini-diner in the main concourse, the American Coffee Shop is great for a snack, or for lunch. It serves up a nice plate of chicken with plantains; if you want to wander and munch at the same time, fresh empanadas filled with chicken, beef, or cheese are always available.

Ramonita's Restaurant For authentic Hispanic Caribbean cuisine, stop by the counter at Ramonita's. Order an exotic dish such as mondongo, mofongo, or alcapurrias de jueyes con camarones. Virgilio Rodriguez, the owner of Ramonita's, can help you choose what to have for lunch and tell you the history of the market.

Food Markets
The Bronx

Arthur Avenue Retail Market

2344 Arthur Avenue at East 187th Street, Belmont, The Bronx
Monday to Saturday, 6 am to 6 pm
(Sundays before Thanksgiving, Christmas, and New Year's Eve)
Metro-North from Grand Central Terminal:
Harlem or New Haven Lines to Fordham Road,
or Hudson Line to University Heights;
or 4, D to Fordham Road then #12 bus heading east;
or 2, 5 to Pelham Parkway then #12 bus heading west

The neighborhood of Belmont in the Bronx is a time capsule of the old Italian neighborhoods that flourished around the city in the last century. It is the best example of a Little Italy in New York these days, now that Little Italy in Manhattan has become smaller and smaller. The Arthur Avenue Retail Market has retained the authenticity of the Old World, its flavors, smells, sights, and sounds.

Arthur Avenue is one of the indoor markets created by Mayor La Guardia in the 1940s to house one hundred pushcart vendors. The push-carts fit neatly side by side in the market, and shoppers would pass by, purchasing potatoes from one cart, tomatoes from the next, and onions from a third. Today there are nine vendors who have expanded over the years to take up multiple spaces. There is a wonderful selection of fresh produce, meat, Italian groceries, prepared foods, and more.

When you walk into the market, the first thing that hits you are the smells, maybe of meat being smoked on the premises, hot tomato sauce being slathered over eggplant parmigiana, or perhaps a whiff of moist tobacco from the cigar rollers at the front entrance. The next sensation is the sound of Paul Anka or Louis Prima crooning over the sound system. Before long, you will be humming "Volare" or "Mambo Italiano" along with everyone else. You will see the old-timers from the neighborhood greeting the vendors in the Neapolitan dialect. Finally, you will sit down at one of the little cafés and sip a frothy cappuccino, perhaps followed by an Italian hero sandwich, with salami, sopressata, and mozzarella on a fresh Italian hero roll.

Families are at the heart of the old neighborhood, and most of the businesses are run by fathers and sons, nephews and uncles, or three brothers or two sisters, who know their customers by name and by food preferences. Many of the shop owners grew up together in the market, and so there is a family feeling inside the market itself. The neighborhood continues to change, but people who know and love the market come back regularly to visit and to stock up on the imported meats, pastas, grapes, nuts, and pastries.

After you have lunch and buy your provisions at the market, you can spend the afternoon wandering into all the Italian groceries, bakeries, pastry shops, and butcher shops along Arthur Avenue. End the day with dinner at one of the local Italian restaurants, many of which get their supplies from the market.

Peter's Meat Market Peter's Meat Market is known for its top-quality veal, free-range chicken, quail, osso buco (veal and beef), and tripe, as well as meatballs, chicken cutlets, and beef or pork bracciole. Owners Peter Servedio and his nephew Mike Rella have owned this butcher shop since it opened in 1970. During the holidays, you'll find veal roast with asparagus and prosciutto, pork roast stuffed with spinach, and provolone and prosciutto wrapped with pancetta.

Liberatore's Garden Joe Liberatore and his son Richard manage this seed and plant shop. This green corner of the market is filled with houseplants, bags of soil, and clay pots, but the biggest draw is imported vegetable seeds from Italy. The Liberatores sell seeds to grow spigariello, broccoli raab, peperoncini, arugula, basil, and more. Joe—known locally as the Mayor of Little Italy—was a teenager pushcart vendor who originally moved into the market under Mayor La Guardia, starting with one small stand selling a few vegetables.

Boiano Foods, Inc. The three Boiano brothers, Anthony, Joe, and Pat, sell fresh fruit, vegetables, and herbs, including seasonal items imported from Italy such as moscato grapes and chestnuts. They also carry nuts that are important ingredients in Italian food, such as hazelnuts and almonds, sold by the scoop. At the height of summer, you can pick up squash blossoms grown by women in the neighborhood. All three brothers know Italian food, and it's not unusual to hear them exchanging recipes with customers.

Mount Carmel Gourmet Food Shop Countless types of pasta grace the shelves of this Italian food shop, from squid-ink spaghetti to tagliatelle al tartuffo. In addition to selling a selection of imported olive oils and balsamic vinegars from Modena, the proprietors, sisters Modesta and Maria Navarra, from the Piemonte region of Italy, prepare gift baskets filled with such delicacies as olives, sun-dried tomatoes, porcini mushrooms, Sicilian oregano, capers, coffee, and more. At the shop, you'll find large hunks of sweet torrone with hazelnuts and other Italian candies and cookies. During the holidays, the counters are stacked with festive boxes of panetone and pandoro, both imported from Italy.

La Casa Grande Tobacco Company (www.lcgcigars. com) La Casa Grande's talented rollers make rich brown and fragrant cigars by hand, using tobacco grown in the Dominican Republic from Cuban seeds, as well as leaves from Honduras, Nicaragua, Mexico, and, interestingly, Connecticut. In addition to making Cuban-style cigars, they have also created blends of their own. La Casa Grande will send a cigar roller to your next party and make custom labels for their cigars for weddings, new babies, companies, or any celebration. You'll find rollers from Casa Grande making cigars at The Grand Havana Room, New York's private cigar club, the last Wednesday of every month. Loyal customers include actors Chazz Palminteri and Vincent Pastore.

Mike's Deli "The Original Arthur Avenue Italian Deli"
(www.arthuravenue.com) Cured sausages and round
mozzarella cheeses are strung across the front of this
deli, cans of imported olive oils are stacked one on top of
the other, and trays of hot foods bubble in sauces at the
counter. The shop extends across the aisle, with barrels
of olives and nuts, as well as a full-service café. The current owner is David Greco, a third-generation shopkeeper
at the market. The first business was a butcher shop run by
his maternal grandparents; his father opened Mike's Deli
in 1951. The deli is a food lover's mecca for fine imported
and locally made Italian foods. David is a talented chef who
has appeared on the Food Network, with Paula Deen and
Bobby Flay (who he beat in an eggplant parm throwdown).

Farmers Markets

Farmers Markets

There are more than fifty farmers markets held each week throughout the city's five boroughs that provide fresh, nutritious, and delicious fruits and vegetables, as well as a surprising number of other food items, to the neighborhoods they serve.

There is a staggering variety at the greenmarkets. You can find staples such as potatoes, lettuce, and tomatoes—but you might find six varieties of potatoes in one stand, eight types of lettuces at another, and dozens of different heirloom tomatoes. Look for free-range chicken and quail eggs; artisanal cheeses; grass-fed beef, turkey, and lamb; pork sausages and bacon; and New York State wines, as well as fresh breads, pastries, cookies, and pretzels. There are always stands selling honeys, jams, jellies, and pickles. You will often see cooking and nutrition demonstrations and local musicians performing on market days.

As I explored many of the farmers markets around the city, I was delighted to find that each market has adapted to the neighborhood it serves. The same farmers go to several different markets during the week, and they know what their customers want to buy in each different neighborhood. Most people frequent the market in their own neighborhood, but it is worth branching out occasionally and exploring the offerings in other parts of town. You'll find tables with a dozen or more different kinds of peppers in Caribbean and Hispanic neighborhoods, and a wider selection of onions, cabbages, and sausages in the market in Williamsburg, which has a large Polish population. Other neighborhoods have many more varieties of leafy greens for their "downtown" clientele.

The Council on the Environment of New York City (www.cenyc.org) manages the majority of the farmers markets in the city. Stop by the council's green tent to pick up a recipe or to find out what special programs are being held at the market. (Markets often sponsor other community activities such as book signings, tastings, recycling, and composting.) The CENYC market managers also accept credit cards at many markets—your card is swiped and you are given you chips for that amount. Pay the farmers with your chips, and they give you your change in cash.

Several innovative and important community programs are worth mentioning. The New Farmer Development Program (NFDP) helps new immigrants become successful local farmers and sell their produce at the greenmarkets. The CENYC also offers youth education programs to help city children learn about agriculture and food production. Many of the markets accept food stamps, in order to help make good nutrition accessible to all.

Smaller organizations run local farmers markets in different parts of the city as well, thus helping ensure that the markets are everywhere they are needed. Community Markets (www.communitymarkets.biz) manages seven markets in the city, as well as eleven markets upstate.

Added Value (www.added-value.org) is a nonprofit organization that turned a rundown playground into a robust community market in Red Hook, Brooklyn. Their latest initiative is an organic farm planted in 2009 on Governors Island, a former military base in the middle of New York Harbor. This three-acre urban farm is linked to the New York Harbor School and will teach teenagers about agriculture, science, and business management. The plan is to open an organic farm stand, and food vendors on the island will use the farm's produce.

This section covers eleven of my favorite markets and profiles many of the farmers you will find at these and other markets. I have selected a mix of the larger and smaller markets in interesting locations, as well as several that take place near the best artisan and flea markets. Many of these markets work together to make it easier and more pleasurable for us to do all of our shopping at markets, whether we are buying fresh beets or a pair of handmade earrings.

Farmers Markets
Manhattan

77th Street Greenmarket

Columbus Avenue at West 77th Street.
Sunday 8 am to 4 pm
1 to 79th Street; B, C to 81st Street-
American Museum of Natural History

It's true what they say about New York: location is everything. This market sets up in one of the Upper West Side's most picturesque locations alongside the Museum of Natural History, a block from Central Park. It is also one of the larger farmers markets, with approximately twenty farmers and other vendors each week.

Strolling beneath the shade of tall and stately London Plane trees, you'll see little old ladies with wheelie carts picking out peaches alongside dads with little kids on their shoulders. Dog walkers trail hopeful hounds with noses sniffing for dropped muffin crumbs.

This Sunday market coincides with the weekly GreenFlea Market, located diagonally across Columbus Avenue in the schoolyard of P.S. 87 (see p.43). During May and October, the market is also enhanced by Crafts on Columbus, an open-air crafts fair sponsored by the American Arts & Crafts Alliance, Inc. (see p.125).

Knoll Krest Farm (www.knollkrestfarm.com) Knoll Krest Farm knows eggs. They raise "free-running hens," on purely vegetarian feed, with no added hormones or antibiotics.

Berkshire Berries (www.berkshireberries.com) Proprietors Mary and David Graves produce and hand-pick the raspberries, blueberries, and strawberries for their jams and jellies from their own back yard. They make savory jellies as well, such as Garlic Jelly and Green Pepper Jelly. One of my favorite market items is their New York City Honey, made from thriving beehives they have placed (with permission) on rooftops all over the city. Just for fun, the next time you watch the movie *You've Got Mail*, see if you can spot their sign at the farmers market where Meg Ryan and Tom Hanks buy flowers and apples.

Valley Shepherd Creamery (www.valleyshepherd.com) True to its name, Valley Shepherd Creamery raises Dutch Friesian milk sheep in New Jersey, a mere fifty-five miles from New York City. Like many of the other farmers in the markets, they raise the lambs hormone- and antibiotic-free. They use traditional methods to make more than twenty-five types of artisanal cheese, which are aged in a cave built into the side of a hill on the farm. Crumbly Ancient Shepherd, richly striated Crema de Blue, and the creamy Shepherd's Cushions are only three of their vast selection.

Martin's Pretzels (www.martinspretzels.com) Martin's sourdough pretzels have been a mainstay in New York's Greenmarkets since 1982. Made by Mennonites in Lancaster County, Pa., many a young New Yorker has soothed their teething pains by sucking on one of these pretzels.

Tamarack Hollow Farm (www.pork.triangul.us) You are walking through the market. You are feeling sleepy. You are craving bacon. It must be Tamarack Hollow Farm's distinct "Bacon Hypnosis" sign that drew you to their tent in the first place. This Vermont-based farm sells organic, pasture-raised chicken, turkey, and pork products, including their famous spicy and smoky bacon. Tamarack's animals are raised cage-free and free-roaming, with no added hormones or antibiotics.

175th Street Greenmarket

West 175th Street and Broadway
Thursday 8 am to 4 pm, June through November
A to 175th Street

Washington Heights runs almost to the northernmost tip of Manhattan island, ending just below Inwood. Many European immigrants settled in this area in the first half of the 1900s, and over time, it has become a primarily Caribbean neighborhood, with residents from the Dominican Republic, Puerto Rico, and Cuba. The market is held on a weekday, and so it is filled with mostly mothers, grandmothers, and children who socialize and enjoy the Latin music that plays throughout the market.

The farmers at this market cater to the culinary culture of the neighborhood. As you emerge from the subway station just across 175th Street, you can smell the cilantro. You can get small bunches of cilantro in all of the other New York City markets, but here, it is sold in bunches so large that you can barely get a hand around them. You will also see eggplants, cabbages, peppers, and other ingredients used in traditional Latin cuisine. There are eight to ten vendors at this market, selling breads and baked goods, cheeses, produce, honey, and juices.

You will also see Plaza de las Americas, another market set up alongside the greenmarket and managed by the Washington Heights-Inwood Local Development Corporation (WHIDC). Vendors sell flea-market type items, as well as imported produce, such as mangoes, plantains, yucca, and coconuts.

Nolasco Farms Sergio Nolasco came from a long family farming tradition in Puebla, Mexico, and has established a thriving farm in Hackettstown, New Jersey. He participates in the New Farmer Development Project through the Council on the Environment of New York City, which helped him establish his farm in the U.S. He knows what his clients want and need. He brings bushels of onions, bunches of fresh herbs, and baskets of yellow squash blossoms, which can be cut up and baked into quesadillas to give them extra nutrients and color.

Millport Dairy Millport Dairy from Lancaster, Pa., sells traditional Pennsylvania Dutch cheeses, made with all-natural unpasteurized milk. Millport produces several types of cheddar, including mild, sharp, and smoked, as well as colby and monterey jack with hot peppers. Rounding out the dairy's offerings are beef sticks and jerky, pickles, and baked goods, the most unusual of which is the rich, moist, and cream-filled whoopee pie, a favorite of local food bloggers.

S. S. & O. Produce Farms S. S. & O. was one of the founding farmers of the New York greenmarkets in 1976. It continues to serve many of the weekly farmers markets around the city. Located in Orange County, N.Y., this farm grows pretty much everything in the way of produce—and a lot of it. You can spot them immediately by their distinctive arrangements of carrots, beets, onions, celery root, and much more.

Abingdon Square Greenmarket

Abingdon Square, West 12th Street at Hudson St.

Saturday 8 am to 2 pm

1, 2, 3, A, C, E to Fourteenth Street, L to Eighth Avenue

Located in the heart of the West Village, this picturesque market is where I can be found every Saturday, carrying my shopping bag and munching on a fresh scone. With upwards of twelve farmers, the tents now wrap almost all the way around Abingdon Square.

After all these years, I know all of the farmers here. They keep me posted on what produce is at peak season, warn me to stock up on things that are near the end of their season, and let me know what they will be bringing to the market next week. They know many of the neighborhood residents, too, including children and dogs. One neighbor buys vegetables from his favorite farmer in the morning and brings her back a delicious lunch he's made from her produce.

Red Jacket Orchards (www.redjacketorchards.com) This orchard in the Finger Lakes region of New York State brings bushels of more than twenty varieties of juicy yellow and red apples, and, in the summer, also brings plums, berries, cherries, apricots, and peaches. Along the side of the stand, in coolers, you'll find bottles of Red Jacket's fresh ciders and nectars including raspberry apple juice and dark cherry stomp.

Consider Bardwell Farm (www.considerbardwellfarm.com) Traveling to the city from Vermont's Champlain Valley, the folks from Consider Bardwell, a cheese-making co-op founded in 1864, bring their award-winning cheeses to many of the farmers markets each week. *Wine Spectator* included the Manchester goat's milk tomme in its 100 Great Cheeses list, and the farms' cheeses consistently win top awards from the American Cheese Society. You can taste samples at the McCarren Park and Carroll Gardens markets as well.

Meredith's Bread (www.meredithsbread.com) Remember my Saturday morning scone? I pick it up at Meredith's Bread, which sells muffins, breads, pies, cookies, and quiches too—more than three hundred varieties, including sugar-free, wheat-free, gluten-free, organic, and made with New York ingredients wherever possible. You'll find Meredith's at products forty-four markets each week.

Lani's Farm (www.lanisfarm.blogspot.com) Baby lettuces from Lani's Farm make for tender salads all week long. The large table covered in summer in red, orange, yellow, and green heirloom tomatoes is one of the most popular spots in the market. If you are looking for unusual vegetables, like edamame, bok choy, different varieties of eggplant, and many more, you may well find them at Lani's stand.

Bowling Green Greenmarket

Broadway at Battery Place

Tuesday and Thursday, 8 am to 5 pm

1 to South Ferry; 4, 5 to Bowling Green

This quaint market is held in an unlikely spot for a farmers market. Situated at the bottom of Manhattan, it is located just outside the historic Bowling Green Park, a small triangular park that is the oldest in the city. Wall Street and the Financial District are a short walk away, and the market is also just outside the front doors of the Smithsonian's National Museum of the American Indian, as well as the not-quite-so-fascinating U.S. Bankruptcy Court.

Migliorelli Farm (www.migliorelli.com) This Hudson Valley farm has been feeding the region since 1933, growing more than 130 kinds of fruits and vegetables. Check the website for a complete listing of everything Migliorelli will be selling each week in the markets.

The Orchards of Concklin (www.theorchardsofconcklin. com) Three tantalizing words are almost all you need to know about The Orchards of Concklin: apple cider donuts. Packed in bags of six, these donuts are moist and cakey on the inside and covered with crunchy crystal sugar and cinnamon on the outside. The other thing you need to know is that the Orchards of Concklin, founded by Nicholas Concklin in 1712, is the eighth oldest family business in the United States.

Union Square Greenmarket

Union Square East, 17th Street and Broadway

Monday, Wednesday, Friday, Saturday 8 am to 6 pm

4, 5, 6, L, N, Q, R, W to 14th Street-Union Square

Union Square is the flagship of New York City's farmers markets, boasting 140 producers each week on two acres of market at the north end of the square. It is also held most frequently—four days a week. Anytime of the day, you will find it bustling.

The best chefs in the city love this market. Danny Meyer, Bobby Flay, Mario Batali—they all sing its praises and buy ingredients for their restaurants and shows from its farmers. It is no coincidence that many of the city's finest restaurants are within a stone's throw of this market. Get there at the crack of dawn to rub shoulders with your favorite celebrity chefs. Union Square is also a favorite of Alice Waters.

The market experience at Union Square is enhanced by the presence of numerous artisans selling handmade crafts seven days a week, as well as the festive holiday market in November and December (See p.31 and p.155).

Below are some of my favorites. Many purveyors listed under other markets also sell their products at Union Square.

Newfield Flower Farm Pick up an armful of bright and cheerful blossoms at Newfield's tent. The freshly cut flowers come from the farm in Gloucester County, New Jersey. Look for sunflowers, lillies, snapdragons, gladiolus, and many more by the stem or in boquets.

Flying Pigs Farm (www.flyingpigsfarm.com) Flying Pigs Farm raises rare heritage breeds: Large Blacks, Glouchestershire Old Spots, and Tamworths. The aim is to create a market for these breeds so that they can be preserved in the U.S. These breeds also produce meat that is moister and more flavorful than current hybrids. You can buy succulent pork chops, spare ribs, and ham steaks. They sell pork shoulder and a plethora of savory sausages. And, of course, they always bring the bacon.

Dancing Ewe Farm (www.dancingewe.com) Specializing in Tuscan-style cheeses, Dancing Ewe sells out of the salty ricotta, flaky pecorino, and tangy caciotta very quickly, so stop here first. Proprietor Jody Somers left veterinary school to study traditional cheese making in Tuscany, where he also met his wife Luisa. Together they raise their sheep in Granville, N.Y. Mario Batali serves Dancing Ewe cheeses at his Italian restaurants: Babbo, Del Posto, Lupa, and Otto.

Beth's Farm Kitchen (www.bethsfarmkitchen.com) After you pick up fresh bread at the market, zip over to Beth's Farm Kitchen for something zesty to spread on it. These handmade jams and chutneys are made from locally grown fruit in an 1850s farmhouse kitchen in the Hudson Valley. You'll find more than ninety flavors, from comfy and familiar strawberry jam for your toast to Blazing Tomato Chutney, which can be "a bit mean and ornery."

Tickle Hill Winery (www.ticklehillwinery.com) Tickle Hill wines are produced on a 42-acre vineyard in the Finger Lakes region of New York State. Check out the funny names of the wines (Grape-Full Red, Tickle Me Pink, Hector Nectar)—methinks they may be testing the product a wee bit too much. Most of the wines are under $10 a bottle

Baker's Bounty (www.bakersbounty.net) Baker's Bounty sets up a charming and complete bakery shop under green tents at the market including Italian breads, baguettes, multigrain and semolina raisin loaves, sesame twists, challah bread, and more. If it's sweets you're after, look for the cookies, scones, macaroons, muffins, and Danish. Seasonal treats, like chocolate chip pumpkin loaf in the fall and peach muffins in the summertime, are also available.

Eve's Cidery (www.evescidery.com) Not in the mood for wine? Try a bottle of Eve's artisanal semi-sweet, dry, or "bone dry" ciders with 10–12% alcohol. The apples are grown in the orchards and fermented in Eve's own cidery. The next time you're invited to someone's house for dinner, bring along a bottle of Eve's Apple Ice Wine—made from frozen apples, with 15% residual sugars; it's perfect with dessert.

Farmers Markets
Brooklyn

Ft. Greene Park Greenmarket

Washington Park *(Note: this is the name of a street)* and
Dekalb Avenue, Ft. Greene
Saturday 8 am to 5 pm
C to Lafayette Avenue; G to Fulton Street; Q, R to Dekalb Avenue

Of all the farmers markets I visited, the Ft. Greene market seems to be one of the happiest. The market came to the neighborhood in 2007, where it was fully embraced by the residents. Neighbors are happy to see "their" farmers every Saturday, and the feeling is mutual.

Ft. Greene Park, designed by Frederick Law Olmsted and Calvert Vaux, who designed both Central Park and Brooklyn's Prospect Park, is a beautiful backdrop for the twenty or more farmers, cheese mongers, and bakers who set up under the shade of majestic 150-year-old black walnut trees.

Joggers and dog walkers come out of the park early in the morning and stop at the market for a bottle of fruit juice, or a fresh muffin for breakfast. The market gets crowded with families and foodies just after 10:00 am. If you are lucky, you will run into the "cookie kids." This brother and sister, probably eight and five years old, bake up a batch of chocolate chip cookies, tape signs to their shoulders ('Cookies for 25 Cents Yum'), and walk around selling the warm cookies to shoppers and farmers alike. You can't help but buy one and give them a dollar for being so cute—and entrepreneurial.

 **Wilklow Farms** (www.wilkloworchards.com) This upstate family farm grows apples, pears, cherries, plums, grapes, gooseberries, blackberries, peaches—and the list goes mouthwateringly on. An entire tent in the summer is dedicated solely to twenty-plus varieties of heirloom tomatoes, which you can sample—each one better than the last. An auntie does all of the baking using fresh ingredients from the farm for her pies, muffins, breads, and donuts. Wilklow has been selling at New York's greenmarkets for more than twenty-five years.

 **Cato Corner Farmstead Cheeses** (www.catocornerfarm.com) Cato Corner's cheeses are made by hand with raw milk from the cows on their Connecticut farm. The cows are hormone-free and graze on pasture grass. Because the cows' diet changes seasonally with the vegetation, the flavor of their milk changes as well. These cheesemakers make cheddars in the summertime and creamier cheeses in the cold months. The names given the cheese may tickle your funny bone (Wise Womanchego, Dairyere).

 **Cayuga Pure Organics** (www.cporganics.com) As if beans and grains weren't healthy enough, Cayuga grows them organically. The farm stand packages pinto, black, red, soy, and navy beans, as well as "hard red" spring wheat and spelt, in resealable paper bags.

Grand Army Plaza Greenmarket

Prospect Park West and Flatbush Avenue

Saturday 8 am to 4 pm

2, 3 to Grand Army Plaza

Brooklyn's flagship farmers market on Grand Army Plaza starts buzzing first thing in the morning and doesn't stop until the tents come down. The Plaza is a main entrance to Prospect Park, Brooklyn's 585-acre sibling to Manhattan's Central Park.

The Saturday farmers market is located just beyond the Soldiers' and Sailors' Arch. Families from nearby Park Slope, Prospect Heights, and Crown Heights neighborhoods come early for their provisions, while bikers, joggers, skaters, and dog walkers come out of the park for a drink and a snack. Brooklyn's most ardent foodies and bloggers keep a close eye on everything that is fresh and new at the market.

With thirty-five farmers and vendors each week, there is much to see, smell, and taste. This market is known for its live music and activities, including family-friendly events, such as pumpkin painting and apple cider pressing in the fall. The market also raffles off reusable bags full of farm products. On some days, you can learn how to filet a fish or make your own pickles. A visit to this market can become an entire afternoon of entertainment.

Mycomedicinals from Madura Farms The most glorious of mushrooms sit in the bins at Madura Farms' Mycomedicinals tent. Whether you are interested in their medicinal properties or their earthy and delicious tastes, you can stock up on Lion's Mane, King Oysters, Shiitakes, and many more. My very favorite is their lacy Maitakes, which I know as "hen of the woods." I learned that yogis have been using a tea made from the mushroom for centuries to deepen meditation; it also lowers the blood pressure.

Rick's Picks (www.rickspicksnyc.com) As much as you may love your standard dill pickles, Rick's Picks' fourteen varieties of sweet, savory, and spicy pickles will broaden your horizons to the farthest reaches of preserved veggies. There are pickled beets, asparagus spears, green beans, okra, and yes, even "kool gherks," Rick's version of your traditional whole dill pickle. You may have already tried Rick's Picks in Whole Foods, Dean & Deluca, and gourmet food shops across the country. You can also talk pickle with founder Rick Field in person at many of the other farmers markets, the Brooklyn Flea, and the New Amsterdam Market.

New York Wine and Grape Foundation
(www.newyorkwines.org) Each week at the market, this organization brings wines from several New York wineries and offers sample tastings. The aim is to create awareness of the state's multiple wine regions, from Lake Erie and Chautauqua, to the Niagra Escarpment, the Finger Lakes, the Hudson River Valley, Long Island, and others. You definitely want to stop by for a chat and a taste—or four—of the fruits of New York State's vines.

Nature's Way Farm (www.natureswayfarm.com) Dedicated beekeepers, the producers at Nature's Way bring their sweet and nutritious products to several markets from their farm in the Finger Lakes. Their honeys have distinctly different flavors, from the milder Wildflower Honey to the deep, rich Buckwheat Honey. They also sell other bee-related products, including bee pollen, propolis tincture, honey soaps, and beeswax candles. For true honey fans, they have honeycomb and gallon jars of honey, which are huge and may require that you take a taxi to get yours home.

Kernan Farms New Jersey farmer Kernie Kernan sells his fresh produce at multiple markets across the city. You will recognize his distinct white signs with hand-drawn pictures of the items they are resting on, with not just prices, but also nutritional information, recipes, and interesting quotes from people like Meryl Streep, who apparently said, "It's bizarre that the produce market is more important to my children's health than the pediatrician." A deep purple eggplant, bright red pepper, dark green zucchini, or rich yellow squash a day will definitely keep the doctor away.

Blue Moon Fish (www.bluemoonfish.com) These local fishermen sell the seafood freshly caught from their boat on eastern Long Island. Their catch varies from season to season, although many varieties are available year round. They have over twenty kinds of fillets, such as codfish, flounder, mackerel, skate, squid, striped bass, swordfish, and tuna. You can also buy whole bonito, herring, sea bass, and sea trout, among others. Head fisherman Alex Villani has been selling in the New York Greenmarkets since 1988 and even met his wife Stephanie at the Union Square market. But that's another story.

$3.00 lb.

Green beans and

$1.80 lb.

$1.50 lb.

Vitamin A Vitamin C Protein. Good source of fiber!
Vitamins A & C!

Zucchini

Try Zucchini Fritters
1½ cup of flour
3/4 tsp. baking powder
3/4 tsp salt
1 cup milk
1 egg, beaten
1 cup of shredded zucchini
Grease for deep frying

In bowl, mix flour, baking powder & salt.
Mix milk, egg & zucchini. Add to dry
ingredients. Mix just until moistened.
Drop by tablespoons, a few at a time,
into heated grease. Fry 3 to 4 minutes
until golden brown. Serve hot. Dip in
ranch dressing or a cheese sauce.

(many more recipes on-line!)

Greenpoint Greenmarket

Union Avenue (N. 12th St. / Driggs Ave.) at McCarren Park

Saturday 8 am to 3 pm

L to Bedford Avenue, G to Nassau Avenue

Greenpoint, Brooklyn, located on the waterfront of the borough's most northerly tip, is a fascinating example of diversity. The neighborhood was primarily Polish after the immigration wave of the early 1900s. In the 1990s, many artists moved into neighboring Williamsburg and Greenpoint as well. The artists attracted young hipsters, who seem to have grown up and are now raising their own families in the neighborhood. This market is great for people watching. And you can still hear Polish spoken among women strolling arm-in-arm and filling up their tote bags.

McCarren Park, located between Greenpoint and Williamsburg, has lawns, ball fields, tennis courts, and even a bocce court. There is a lot going on in this 35-acre park each weekend, including the Artists and Fleas Outdoor Market in the summertime (p.77). Every Saturday, residents from both neighborhoods frequent this lower-key yet vibrant farmers market to buy fresh food from the sixteen farmers who put up their tents.

Garden of Eve (www.gardenofevefarm.com) Garden of Eve is a certified organic farm in Aquebogue, N.Y. The farm sends bushels of fruits and vegetables to the Greenpoint market each week, and if you get there early, you can pick up farm-fresh eggs and flowers, too.

Osczepinski Farms Osczepinski Farms sells its produce at several markets around the city, and their distinct presentation using wooden crates sets them apart visually. You can easily admire the orange carrots, magenta beets, and white onions, which are arranged in neat stacks.

Cranberry Hall Farm This Cookstown, N.J., farm brings crates of farm-fresh produce to the market. It is so fresh that you can see rich brown dirt still clinging to green, red, and purple eggplants, or basketball-size watermelons. You can whip up amazing vegetable dishes with picks from this farmstand. Or you can bite into a green pepper for lunch and be on your way (wipe off the dirt first).

Arcadian Pastures (www.arcadianpastures.com)
Arcadian Pastures raises heritage breeds on a grass-fed, certified organic, family farm. These breeds are indeed the heritage of American agriculture, unaltered by genetic engineering, and farms like Arcadian Pastures are committed to creating and maintaining a market for them to ensure that they are around for future generations. Their wooden display bins contain succulent cuts of beef, lamb, pork, chicken, and rabbit. They also have sausages and ham, favorites among the Polish neighbors and, frankly, anyone with taste buds.

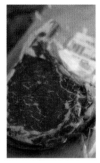

Farmers Markets
The Bronx

Poe Park Greenmarket • 243

Poe Park Greenmarket

192nd Street (Grand Concourse / Valentine Ave.), Bronx

Tuesday 8 am to 3 pm, July through November

4, D to Kingsbridge Road or Fordham Road

The final home of American author Edgar Allan Poe—his tiny cottage and darling garden—still sits in Poe Park in the Bronx. According to the Bronx County Historical Society, Poe wrote many of his most important works in this cottage, including "The Bells," "Eureka," and "Annabel Lee." A new Visitors Center was recently built to provide information and tours about the author and his life in the cottage. You can visit www.nyc govparks.org for information about Poe Park.

This midweek farmers market takes place at the southern end of the park in the Bedford Park neighborhood. The area is mostly Hispanic, although there are people from all over the world living there. This is one of the busiest markets in the city. Here, I learned how to make a grated raw beet and apple salad at a cooking demonstration, conducted in Spanish by the CENYC staff and volunteers. Because this market takes place on a school day, you may see groups of school kids on field trips, meeting the farmers, and learning about agriculture and nutrition.

There are ten to twelve farmers and vendors at this market each week, including at least two from the New Farmer Development Program. Nolasco Farms and Mimomex Farm are the stalls to visit if you are looking for a special ingredient for a Latin American recipe, especially peppers; you can find poblano, serrano, longhot, jalapeño, sweet, bell, wax, cherry bomb, and even more at the Poe Park market.

RodriMex Farms RodriMex cultivates typical Mexican vegetables that are probably not so easy to find in your local grocery store. You can find fresh epazote at proprietor Martin Rodriguez's stall, as well as bushels of tender squash blossoms at the height of summer, verdolaga (purslane), tomatillos, and cilantro.

Not Just Rugelach (www.notjustrugelach.com) Not Just Rugelach, headquartered in Kearny, N.J., makes a vast array of mouthwatering baked goods. They bake over a dozen kinds of breads, plus muffins, turnovers, and buttery croissants. They also sell large focaccia slices and knishes that are a meal in and of themselves. But their sweets are my weakness, from the marble cake to the fresh chocolate chip cookies, not to mention the cinnamon buns, brownies, and jelly donuts. And, truth be told, they could sell me just their moist and flaky rugelach, and I'd keep going back for more.

Farmers Markets
Queens

Jackson Heights Greenmarket

34th Avenue at 77th Street

Sunday 8 am to 3 pm, June through November

E, F, G, R to Jackson Heights-Roosevelt Avenue

Jackson Heights is one of the most vibrant and diverse neighborhoods in New York City. It is known as an Indian neighborhood, where you can get authentic and delicious Indian food, shop in Indian stores, and buy curry in five-pound bags. Many people from the Indian community shop at the farmers market for fresh vegetables, and get most of their staple food items in the nearby Indian groceries, which are worth exploring when you are in Queens.

At the market you will see mostly people of Hispanic and Indian descent, including women wearing brightly colored saris. In recent years, many of the younger hipsters and families who were priced out of Brooklyn moved to Jackson Heights, and they frequent the market as well. The market has fourteen farmers and vendors each week and takes place on the sidewalk around Travers Park.

Tello's Green Farm Tello's Green Farm sells fresh eggs from free-range, antibiotic-free chickens: white, brown, and small pullet eggs from young birds. If you get there early, you might be able to pick up some Martha Stewar-tesque little blue-green eggs from their Araucana chick-ens—blow out the insides, and place the decorative shells in a pretty bowl, just like Martha would.

DiPaola Turkey Farm This family farm in New Jersey brings turkey breasts and turkey sausages to market each week. The ground turkey comes plain or with sweet or hot spices, all of which can be quickly browned with an onion and tomato sauce for a healthy, delectable pasta sauce. There's a camping stove kept burning at the stand, cooking a constant stream of hot and tasty samples.

Phillips Farms (www.phillipsfarms.com) Phillips Farms in Milford, N.J., grows luscious fruit brought to the market both fresh and canned. Pears, berries, plums, peaches, and apples are sweet and delicious, even sweeter when turned into jams and fruit spreads (sweetened with grape juice instead of sugar). Phillips uses nearly a pound of fruit per jar, which means one tablespoon of jam equals one fruit serving. I like that math.

Multiple Market Itineraries

Multiple Market Itineraries

Want to spend an entire day at New York City markets? My sister Andrea (nickname "Turbo") likes to optimize a day by visiting as many markets as she possibly can, so I have designed several itineraries that will take fellow turbo shoppers to all the markets in a particular part of town. These routes are not for the faint of heart; you will need provisions: comfy shoes, sunblock, and a shopping bag filled with energy and enthusiasm for the hunt. You can walk these routes in either direction.

Markets of Lower Manhattan
Saturday and Sunday

This route will take you from the Lower East Side, up into Nolita, across the top of Soho, to Greenwich Village. Essex Street Market is a food market where you can grab a great cup of coffee and fill your pockets with snacks for the road. Old St. Patrick's, St. Anthony's, and Our Lady of Pompeii are all sidewalk markets where craftspeople sell handmade items. Young Designers is a sartorial dream come true, and Billy's offers an ever-changing eclectic collection of antiques and props.

- Essex Street Market, page 171
- Old St. Patrick's Cathedral Market, page 57
- Young Designers Market, page 69
- Billy's Antiques and Props, page 35
- St. Anthony's Outdoor Market, page 65
- Our Lady of Pompeii Crafts Market, page 61

Manhattan's East Side Markets

Saturday and Sunday

(Note: The East 67th Street Market is open only on Saturday.)

Spend a day exploring the east side of Manhattan, wandering through tony neighborhoods and into iconic landmarks Grand Central Terminal and Union Square. You will visit two classic flea and antiques markets and the delectable food market at Grand Central Station, and end up at the artisan and farmers markets in Union Square. This route is too long for all but the most intrepid to walk, but all of the destinations are within a reasonable distance from the 4, 5, and 6 subway lines.

- East 67th Street Market, page 37
- Grand Central Market, page 177
- Antiques Garage, page 25
- Artists at Union Square, page 31
- Union Square Greenmarket, page 221

Williamsburg and Greenpoint, Brooklyn Markets

Saturday and Sunday

Williamsburg and Greenpoint are filled with immigrant history, old and new, and you can spend a day wandering through the markets there. Visit all three locations of Artists and Fleas, as well as the Greenpoint/McCarran Park Greenmarket on Saturdays in season. The Meeker Avenue Flea Market is nearby, and you can visit the Moore Street Market for some Hispanic and Caribbean fare.

- Artists and Fleas (Indoor Artists and Designers Market, Vintage Market, Market in McCarren Park), page 77
- Meeker Avenue Flea Market, page 111
- Moore Street Market/La Marqueta, page 189

Holiday Season Along Fifth Avenue

Daily in December

The concrete jungle becomes warm and cozy, with twinkling lights, shop window decorations, and, of course, incredible shopping. This route takes you to two traditional holiday markets and past the wondrous sites on Fifth Avenue. Dress warmly.

Start at the Columbus Circle Holiday Market, and then stroll through Central Park, or take a hansom carriage ride across to Fifth Avenue. Don't miss the holiday windows at Bergdorf Goodman and Saks Fifth Avenue, and the Christmas tree at Rockefeller Center. The next stop is the Holiday Fair at Grand Central, where you can also see the New York Transit Museum's holiday train. Pick up something warm and delicious for lunch at the Grand Central Market, and continue your stroll downtown to the see the festive windows at Macy's, stopping by the holiday market at Bryant Park, if time permits.

- Columbus Circle Holiday Market, page 149
- Grand Central Terminal Holiday Fair, page 151
- Grand Central Market, page 177
- The Holiday Shops at Bryant Park, page 157

Index

About The Author

After receiving her MA at The Johns Hopkins University, Karen E. Seiger spent the first part of her career focusing on international aid and development in Latin America and Africa. She moved to New York City in 2000 with her husband, where she changed careers to focus on international marketing and communications at American Express, and then as an independent business consultant and writer. She volunteers as a tour guide of the World Trade Center Site. When she's home, her family never misses the Saturday morning farmers market at Abingdon Square in the West Village.